ISBN 0-8373-6648-8

DANTES-48

Rudman's Question and Answer

DANTES SUBJECT STANDARDIZED TESTS

Subject Examination In . . .

PERSONNEL/HUMAN RESOURCE MANAGEMENT

Questions and Answers

NATIONAL LEARNING CORP
212 MICHAEL DRIVE, SYOSSET, NEW YORK

National Learning Corporation

212 Michael Drive, Syosset, New York 11791

(516) 921-8888
(800) 645-6337
FAX: (516) 921-8743
www.passbooks.com
sales @ passbooks.com
info @ passbooks.com

PRINTED IN THE UNITED STATES OF AMERICA

PASSBOOK®

NOTICE

This book is *SOLELY* intended for, is sold *ONLY* to, and its use is *RESTRICTED* to *individual*, bona fide applicants or candidates who qualify by virtue of having seriously filed applications for appropriate license, certificate, professional and/or promotional advancement, higher school matriculation, scholarship, or other legitimate requirements of educational and/or governmental authorities.

This book is *NOT* intended for use, class instruction, tutoring, training, duplication, copying, reprinting, excerption, or adaptation, etc., by:

(1) Other Publishers

(2) Proprietors and/or Instructors of "Coaching" and/or Preparatory Courses

(3) Personnel and/or Training Divisions of commercial, industrial, and governmental organizations

(4) Schools, colleges, or universities and/or their departments and staffs, including teachers and other personnel

(5) Testing Agencies or Bureaus

(6) Study groups which seek by the purchase of a single volume to copy and/or duplicate and/or adapt this material for use by the group as a whole without having purchased individual volumes for each of the members of the group

(7) Et al.

Such persons would be in violation of appropriate Federal and State statutes.

PROVISION OF LICENSING AGREEMENTS. — Recognized educational commercial, industrial, and governmental institutions and organizations, and others legitimately engaged in educational pursuits, including training, testing, and measurement activities, may address a request for a licensing agreement to the copyright owners, who will determine whether, and under what conditions, including fees and charges, the materials in this book may be used by them. In other words, a licensing facility *exists* for the legitimate use of the material in this book on other than an individual basis. However, it is asseverated and affirmed here that the materials in this book *CANNOT* be used without the receipt of the express permission of such a licensing agreement from the Publishers.

NATIONAL LEARNING CORPORATION
212 Michael Drive
Syosset, New York 11791

Inquiries re licensing agreements should be addressed to:
The President
National Learning Corporation
212 Michael Drive
Syosset, New York 11791

PASSBOOK SERIES®

THE *PASSBOOK SERIES®* has been created to prepare applicants and candidates for the ultimate academic battlefield – the examination room.

At some time in our lives, each and every one of us may be required to take an examination – for validation, matriculation, admission, qualification, registration, certification, or licensure.

Based on the assumption that every applicant or candidate has met the basic formal educational standards, has taken the required number of courses, and read the necessary texts, the *PASSBOOK SERIES®* furnishes the one special preparation which may assure passing with confidence, instead of failing with insecurity. Examination questions – together with answers – are furnished as the basic vehicle for study so that the mysteries of the examination and its compounding difficulties may be eliminated or diminished by a sure method.

This book is meant to help you pass your examination provided that you qualify and are serious in your objective.

The entire field is reviewed through the huge store of content information which is succinctly presented through a provocative and challenging approach – the question-and-answer method.

A climate of success is established by furnishing the correct answers at the end of each test.

You soon learn to recognize types of questions, forms of questions, and patterns of questioning. You may even begin to anticipate expected outcomes.

You perceive that many questions are repeated or adapted so that you can gain acute insights, which may enable you to score many sure points.

You learn how to confront new questions, or types of questions, and to attack them confidently and work out the correct answers.

You note objectives and emphases, and recognize pitfalls and dangers, so that you may make positive educational adjustments.

Moreover, you are kept fully informed in relation to new concepts, methods, practices, and directions in the field.

You discover that you are actually taking the examination all the time: you are preparing for the examination by "taking" an examination, not by reading extraneous and/or supererogatory textbooks.

In short, this PASSBOOK®, used directedly, should be an important factor in helping you to pass your test.

DANTES Subject Standardized Tests

INTRODUCTION

The DANTES (Defense Activity for Non-Traditional Education Support) subject standardized tests are comprehensive college and graduate level examinations given by the Armed Forces, colleges and graduate schools as end-of-subject course evaluation final examinations or to obtain college equivalency credits in the various subject areas tested.

The DANTES Examination Program enables students to obtain college credit for what they have learned on the job, through self-study, personal interest, correspondence courses or by any other means. It is used by colleges and universities to award college credit to students who demonstrate that they know as much as students completing an equivalent college course. It is a cost-efficient, time-saving way for students to use their knowledge to accomplish their educational goals.

Most schools accept the American Council on Education (ACE) recommendations for the minimum score required and the amount of credit awarded, but not all schools do. Be sure to check the policy regarding the score level required for credit and the number of credits to be awarded.

Not all tests are accepted by all institutions. Even when a test is accepted by an institution, it may not be acceptable for every program at that institution. Before considering testing, ascertain the acceptability of a specific test for a particular course.

Colleges and universities that administer DANTES tests may administer them to any applicant – or they may administer the tests only to students registered at their institution. Decisions about who will be allowed to test are made by the school. Students should contact the test center to determine current policies and schedules for DANTES testing.

Colleges and universities authorized to administer DANTES tests usually do so throughout the calendar year. Each school sets its own fee for test administration and establishes its own testing schedule. Contact the representative at the administering school directly to make arrangements for testing.

Checklist

For Students

- ✓ Visit **www.getcollegecredit.com** to obtain a list of tests, fact sheets, test preparation materials, participating colleges and universities, and much more.
- ✓ Contact your school advisor to confirm that the DSST you selected will fit into your curriculum.
- ✓ Consult the ***DSST Candidate Information Bulletin*** for answers to specific questions.
- ✓ Contact the test site to schedule your test.
- ✓ Prepare for your examination by using the fact sheet as a guide.
- ✓ Take the test.

If you would like a score report sent to your college or university, it is a good idea to bring the four-digit code with you. You must write the DSST Test Center Code for that institution on your answer sheet at the time of testing. DSST Test Center Codes are noted in the DSST Participating Colleges and Universities listing on the Web site.

If you prefer to send a score report to an institution at a later date, there is a transcript fee of $20 for each transcript ordered.

Thomson Prometric
DSST Program
2000 Lenox Drive, Third Floor
Lawrenceville, NJ 08648

Toll-free: 877-471-9860
609-895-5011

E-mail: pnj-dsst@thomson.com

MAKING A COLLEGE DEGREE WITHIN YOUR REACH

Today, there are many educational alternatives to the classroom—you can learn from your job, your reading, your independent study, and special interests you pursue. You may already have learned the subject matter covered by some college-level courses.

The DSST Program is a nationally recognized testing program that gives you the opportunity to receive college credit for learning acquired outside the traditional college classroom. Colleges and universities throughout the United States administer the program, developed by Thomson Prometric, year-round. Annually, over 90,000 DSSTs are administered to individuals who are interested in continuing their education. Take advantage of the DSST testing program; it speeds the educational process and provides the flexibility adults need, making earning a degree more feasible.

Since requirements differ from college to college, please check with the credit-awarding institution before taking a DSST. More than 1,800 colleges and universities currently award credit for DSSTs, and the number is growing every day. You can choose from 37 test titles in the areas of Social Science, Business, Mathematics, Applied Technology, Humanities, and Physical Science. A brief description of each examination is found on the pages that follow.

Reach Your Career Goals Through DSSTs

Use DSSTs to help you earn your degree, get a promotion, or simply demonstrate that you have college-level knowledge in subjects relevant to your work.

Save Time...

You don't have to sit through classes when you have previously acquired the knowledge or experience for most of what is being taught and can learn the rest yourself. You might be able to bypass introductory-level courses in subject areas you already know.

Save Money...

DSSTs save you money because the classes you bypass by earning credit through the DSST Program are classes you won't have to pay for on your way to earning your degree. You can use the money instead to take more advanced courses that can be more challenging and rewarding.

Improve Your Chances for Admission to College

Each college has its own admission policies; however, having passing scores for DSSTs on your transcript can provide strong evidence of how well you can perform at the college level.

Gain Confidence Performing at a College Level

Many adults returning to college find that lack of confidence is often the greatest hurdle to overcome. Passing a DSST demonstrates your ability to perform on a college level.

Make Up for Courses You May Have Missed

You may be ready to graduate from college and find that you are a few credits short of earning your degree. By using semester breaks, vacation time, or leisure time to study independently, you can prepare to take one or more DSSTs, fulfill your academic requirements, and graduate on time.

If You Cannot Attend Regularly Scheduled Classes...

If your lifestyle or responsibilities prevent you from attending regularly scheduled classes, you can earn your college degree from a college offering an external degree program. The DSST Program allows you to earn your degree by study and experience outside the traditional classroom.

Many colleges and universities offer external degree or distance learning programs. For additional information, contact the college you plan to attend or:

Center for Lifelong Learning
American Council on Education
One DuPont Circle NW, Suite 250
Washington, DC 20036
202-939-9475
www.acenet.edu
(Select "Center for Lifelong Learning" under "Programs & Services" for more information)

Fact Sheets

For each test, there is a Fact Sheet that outlines the topics covered by each test and includes a list of sample questions, a list of recommended references of books that would be useful for review, and the number of credits awarded for a passing score as recommended by the American Council on Education (ACE). *Please note that some schools require scores that are higher than the minimum ACE-recommended passing score.* It is suggested that you check with your college or university to determine what score they require in order to earn credit. You can obtain Fact Sheets by:

- Downloading them from www.getcollegecredit.com
- E-mailing a request to pnj-dsst@thomson.com
- Completing a Candidate Publications Order Form

DSST Online Practice Tests

DSST online practice tests contain items that reflect a *partial range of difficulty* identified in the Content Outline section on each Fact Sheet. There is an online DSST Practice Test in the following categories:

- Mathematics
- Social Science
- Business
- Physical Science
- Applied Technology
- Humanities

Although the online DSST Practice Test questions do not indicate the full range of difficulty you would find in an actual DSST test, they will help you assess your knowledge level. Each online DSST Practice Test can be purchased by visiting www.getcollegecredit.com and clicking on DSST Practice Exams.

TAKING DSST EXAMINATIONS

Earning College Credit for DSST Examinations

To find out if the college of your choice awards credit for passing DSST scores, contact the admissions office or counseling and testing office. The college can also provide information on the scores required for awarding credit, the number of credit hours awarded, and any courses that can be bypassed with satisfactory scores.

It is important that you contact the institution of your choice as early as possible since credit-awarding policies differ among colleges and universities.

Where to Take DSSTs

DSSTs are administered at colleges and universities nationwide. Each location determines the frequency and scheduling of test administrations. To obtain the most current list of participating DSST colleges and universities:

- Visit and download the information from www.getcollegecredit.com
- E-mail pnj-dsst@thomson.com

Scheduling Your Examination

Please be aware that some colleges and universities provide DSST testing services to enrolled students only. After you have selected a college or university that administers DSSTs, you will need to contact them to schedule your test date.

The fee to take a DSST is $60 per test. This fee entitles you to two score reports after the test is scored. One will be sent directly to you and the other will be sent to the college or university that you designate on your answer sheet. You may pay the test fee with a certified check or U.S. money order made payable to Thomson Prometric or you may charge the test fee to your Visa, MasterCard or American Express credit card. Note: The credit card statement will reflect a charge from Thomson Prometric for all DSST examinations. *(Declined credit card charges will be assessed an additional $25 processing fee.)*

In addition, the test site may also require a test administration fee for each examination, to be paid directly to the institution. Contact the test site to determine its administration fee and payment policy.

Other Testing Arrangements

If you are unable to find a participating DSST college or university in your area, you may want to contact the testing office of a local accredited college or university to determine whether a representative from that office will agree to administer the test(s) for you.

The school's representative should then contact the DSST Program at 866-794-3497 to arrange for this administration. If you are unable to locate a test site, contact Thomson Prometric for assistance at pnj-dsst@thomson.com or 866-794-3497.

Testing Accommodations for Students with Disabilities

Thomson Prometric is committed to serving test takers with disabilities by providing services and reasonable testing accommodations as set forth in the provisions of the *Americans with Disabilities Act* (ADA). If you have a disability, as prescribed by the ADA, and require special testing services or arrangements, please contact the test administrator at the test site. You will be asked to submit to the test administrator documentation of your disability and your request for special accommodations. The test administrator will then forward your documentation along with your request for testing accommodations to Thomson Prometric for approval.

Please submit your request as far in advance of your test date as possible so that the necessary accommodations can be made. Only test takers with documented disabilities are eligible for special accommodations.

On the Day of the Examination

It is important to review this information and to have the correct identification present on the day of the examination:

• Arrive on time as a courtesy to the test administrator.

• Bring a valid form of government-issued identification that includes a current photo and your signature (acceptable documents include a driver's license, passport, state-issued identification card or military identification). *Anyone who fails to present valid identification will not be allowed to test.*

• Bring several No. 2 (soft-lead) sharpened pencils with good erasers, a watch, and a black pen if you will be writing an essay.

• Do not bring books or papers.

• Do not bring an alarm watch that beeps, a telephone, or a phone beeper into the testing room.

• The use of nonprogrammable calculators, slide rules, scratch paper and/or other materials is permitted for some of the tests.

DSST SCORING POLICIES

Your DSST examination scores are reported only to you, unless you request that they be sent elsewhere. If you want your scores sent to your college, you must provide the correct DSST code number of the school on your answer sheet at the time you take the test. See the *DSST Directory of Colleges and Universities* on the Web site www.getcollegecredit.com.

If your institution is not listed, contact Thomson Prometric at 866-794-3497 to establish a code number. (Some schools may require a student to be enrolled prior to receiving a score report.)

Receiving Your Score Report

Allow approximately four weeks after testing to receive your score report.

Calling DSST Customer Service before the required four-week score processing time has elapsed will not expedite the processing of your scores. Due to privacy and security requirements, scores will not be reported to students over the telephone under any circumstance.

Scoring of Principles of Public Speaking Speeches

The speech portion of the *Principles of Public Speaking* examination will be sent to speech raters who are faculty members at accredited colleges that currently teach or have previously taught the course. Scores for the *Principles of Public Speaking* examination are available six to eight weeks from receipt by Thomson Prometric. If you take the *Principles of Public Speaking* examination and fail (either the objective, speech portion, or both), you must follow the retesting policy waiting period of six months (180 days) before retaking the entire exam.

Essays

The essays for *Ethics in America* and *Technical Writing* are optional and thus are not scored by raters. The essays are forwarded to the college or university that you designate, along with your score report, for their use in determining the award of credit. Before taking the *Ethics in America* or *Technical Writing* examinations, check with your college or university to determine whether the essay is required.

NOTE: *Principles of Public Speaking* speech topic cassette tapes and essays are kept on file at Thomson Prometric for one year from the date of administration.

How to Get Transcripts

There is a $20 fee for each transcript you request. Payment must be in the form of a certified check, U.S. money order payable to Thomson Prometric, or credit card. Personal checks and debit cards are NOT an acceptable method of payment. One transcript may include scores for one or more examinations taken. To request a transcript, download the Transcript Order Form from www.getcollegecredit.com.

DESCRIPTION OF THE DSST EXAMINATIONS

Mathematics

• **Fundamentals of College Algebra** covers mathematical concepts such as fundamental algebraic operations; linear, absolute value; quadratic equations, inequalities, radials, exponents and logarithms, factoring polynomials and graphing. The use of a nonprogrammable, handheld calculator is permitted.

• **Principles of Statistics** tests the understanding of the various topics of statistics, both qualitatively and quantitatively, and the ability to apply statistical methods to solve a variety of problems. The topics included in this test are descriptive statistics; correlation and regression; probability; chance models and sampling and tests of significance. The use of a nonprogrammable, handheld calculator is permitted.

Social Science

• **Art of the Western World** deals with the history of art during the following periods: classical; Romanesque and Gothic; early Renaissance; high Renaissance, Baroque; rococo; neoclassicism and romanticism; realism, impressionism and post-impressionism; early twentieth century; and post-World War II.

• **Western Europe Since 1945** tests the knowledge of basic facts and terms and the understanding of concepts and principles related to the areas of the historical background of the aftermath of the Second World War and rebuilding of Europe; national political systems; issues and policies in Western European societies; European institutions and processes; and Europe's relations with the rest of the world.

• **An Introduction to the Modern Middle East** emphasizes core knowledge (including geography, Judaism, Christianity, Islam, ethnicity); nineteenth-century European impact; twentieth-century Western influences; World Wars I and II; new nations; social and cultural changes (1900-1960) and the Middle East from 1960 to present.

• **Human/Cultural Geography** includes the Earth and basic facts (coordinate systems, maps, physiography, atmosphere, soils and vegetation, water); culture and environment, spatial processes (social processes, modern economic systems, settlement patterns, political geography); and regional geography.

• **Rise and Fall of the Soviet Union** covers Russia under the Old Regime; the Revolutionary Period; New Economic Policy; Pre-war Stalinism; The Second World War; Post-war Stalinism; The Khrushchev Years; The Brezhnev Era; and reform and collapse.

• **A History of the Vietnam War** covers the history of the roots of the Vietnam War; the First Vietnam War (1946-1954); pre-war developments (1954-1963); American involvement in the Vietnam War; Tet (1968); Vietnamizing the War (1968-1973); Cambodia and Laos; peace; legacies and lessons.

• **The Civil War and Reconstruction** covers the Civil War from presecession (1861) through Reconstruction. It includes causes of the war; secession; Fort Sumter; the war in the east and in the west; major battles; the political situation; assassination of Lincoln; end of the Confederacy; and Reconstruction.

• **Foundations of Education** includes topics such as contemporary issues in education; past and current influences on education (philosophies, democratic ideals, social/economic influences); and the interrelationships between contemporary issues and influences.

• **Life-span Developmental Psychology** covers models and theories; methods of study; ethical issues; biological development; perception, learning and memory; cognition and language; social, emotional, and personality development; social behaviors, family life cycle, extrafamilial settings; singlehood and cohabitation; occupational development and retirement; adjustment to life stresses; and bereavement and loss.

• **Drug and Alcohol Abuse** includes such topics as drug use in society; classification of drugs; pharmacological principles; alcohol (types, effects of, alcoholism); general principles and use of sedative hypnotics, narcotic analgesics, stimulants, and hallucinogens; other drugs (inhalants, steroids); and prevention/treatment.

• **General Anthropology** deals with anthropology as a discipline; theoretical perspectives; physical anthropology; archaeology; social organization; economic organization; political organization; religion; and modernization and application of anthropology.

• **Introduction to Law Enforcement** includes topics such as history and professional movement of law enforcement; overview of the U.S. criminal justice system; police systems in the U.S.; police organization, management, and issues; and U.S. law and precedents.

• **Criminal Justice** deals with criminal behavior (crime in the U.S., theories of crime, types of crime); the criminal justice system (historical origins, legal foundations, due process); police; the court system (history and organization, adult court system, juvenile court, pre-trial and post-trial processes); and corrections.

• **Fundamentals of Counseling** covers historical development (significant influences and people); counselor roles and functions; the counseling relationship; and theoretical approaches to counseling.

Business

• **Principles of Finance** deals with financial statements and planning; time value of money; working capital management; valuation and characteristics; capital budgeting; cost of capital; risk and return; and international financial management. The use of a nonprogrammable, handheld calculator is permitted.

• **Principles of Financial Accounting** includes topics such as general concepts and principles, accounting cycle and classification; transaction analysis; accruals and deferrals; cash and internal control; current accounts; long- and short-term liabilities; capital stock; and financial statements. The use of a nonprogrammable, handheld calculator is permitted.

• **Human Resource Management** covers general employment issues; job analysis; training and development; performance appraisals; compensation issues; security issues; personnel legislation and regulation; labor relations and current issues; an overview of the Human Resource Management Field; Human Resource Planning; Staffing; training and development; compensation issues; safety and health; employee rights and discipline; employment law; labor relations and current issues and trends.

• **Organizational Behavior** deals with the study of organizational behavior (scientific approaches, research designs, data collection methods); individual processes and characteristics; interpersonal and group processes and characteristics; organizational processes and characteristics; and change and development processes.

• **Principles of Supervision** deals with the roles and responsibilities of the supervisor; management functions (planning, organization and staffing, directing at the supervisory level); and other topics (legal issues, stress management, union environments, quality concerns).

• **Business Law II** covers topics such as sales of goods; debtor and creditor relations; business organizations; property; and commercial paper.

• **Introduction to Computing** includes topics such as history and technological generations; hardware/software; applications to information technology; program development; data management; communications and connectivity; and computing and society. The use of a nonprogrammable, handheld calculator is permitted.

• **Management Information Systems** covers systems theory, analysis and design of systems, hardware and software; database management; telecommunications; management of the MIS functional area and informational support.

• **Introduction to Business** deals with economic issues affecting business; international business; government and business; forms of business ownership; small business, entrepreneurship and franchise; management process; human resource management; production and operations; marketing management; financial management; risk management and insurance; and management and information systems.

• **Money and Banking** covers the role and kinds of money; commercial banks and other financial intermediaries; central banking and the Federal Reserve system; money and macroeconomics activity; monetary policy in the U.S.; and the international monetary system.

• **Personal Finance** includes topics such as financial goals and values; budgeting; credit and debt; major purchases; taxes; insurance; investments; and retirement and estate planning. The use of auxiliary materials, such as calculators and slide rules, is NOT permitted.

• **Business Mathematics** deals with basic operations with integers, fractions, and decimals; round numbers; ratios; averages; business graphs; simple interest; compound interest and annuities; net pay and deductions; discounts and markups; depreciation and net worth; corporate securities; distribution of ownership; and stock and asset turnover.

Physical Science

• **Astronomy** covers the history of astronomy, celestial mechanics; celestial systems; astronomical instruments; the solar system; nature and evolution; the galaxy; the universe; determining astronomical distances; and life in the universe.

• **Here's to Your Health** covers mental health and behavior; human development and relationships; substance abuse; fitness and nutrition; risk factors, disease, and disease prevention; and safety, consumer awareness, and environmental concerns.

• **Environment and Humanity** deals with topics such as ecological concepts (ecosystems, global ecology, food chains and webs); environmental impacts; environmental management and conservation; and political processes and the future.

• **Principles of Physical Science I** includes physics: Newton's Laws of Motion; energy and momentum; thermodynamics; wave and optics; electricity and magnetism; chemistry: properties of matter; atomic theory and structure; and chemical reactions.

• **Physical Geology** covers Earth materials; igneous, sedimentary, and metamorphic rocks; surface processes (weathering, groundwater, glaciers, oceanic systems, deserts and winds, hydrologic cycle); internal Earth processes; and applications (mineral and energy resources, environmental geology).

Applied Technology

• **Technical Writing** covers topics such as theory and practice of technical writing; purpose, content, and organizational patterns of common types of technical documents; elements of various technical reports; and technical editing. Students have the option to write a short essay on one of the technical topics provided. Thomson Prometric will not score the essay; however, for determining the award of credit, a copy of the essay will be forwarded to the college or university you've designated along with the score report or transcript.

Humanities

• **Ethics in America** deals with ethical traditions (Greek views, Biblical traditions, moral law, consequential ethics, feminist ethics); ethical analysis of issues arising in interpersonal and personal-societal relationships and in professional and occupational roles; and relationships between ethical traditions and the ethical analysis of situations. Students have the option to write an essay to analyze a morally problematic situation in terms of issues relevant to a decision and arguments for alternative positions. Thomson Prometric will not score the essay; however, for determining the award of credit, a copy of the essay will be forwarded to the college or university you've designated along with the score report or transcript.

• **Introduction to World Religions** covers topics such as dimensions and approaches to religion; primal religions; Hinduism; Buddhism; Confucianism; Taoism; Judaism; Christianity; and Islam.

• **Principles of Public Speaking** consists of two parts: Part One consists of multiple-choice questions covering considerations of Principles of Public Speaking; audience analysis; purposes of speeches; structure/organization; content/supporting materials; research; language and style; delivery; communication apprehension; listening and feedback; and criticism and evaluation. Part Two requires the student to record an impromptu persuasive speech that will be scored.

FREQUENTLY ASKED QUESTIONS ABOUT DSSTs

In order to pass the test, must I study from one of the recommended references?

The recommended references are a listing of books that were being used as textbooks in college courses of the same or similar title at the time the test was developed. Appropriate textbooks for study are not limited to those listed in the fact sheet. If you wish to obtain study resources to prepare for the examination, you may reference either the current edition of the listed titles or textbooks currently used at a local college or university for the same class title. It is recommended that you reference more than one textbook on the topics outlined in the fact sheet. You should begin by checking textbook content against the content outline included on the front page of the DSST fact sheet before selecting textbooks that cover the text content from which to study. Textbooks may be found at the campus bookstore of a local college or university offering a course on the subject.

Is there a penalty for guessing on the tests?

There is no penalty for guessing on DSSTs, so you should mark an answer for each question.

How much time will I have to complete the test?

Many DSSTs can be completed within 90 minutes; however, additional time can be allowed if necessary.

What should I do if I find a test question irregularity?

Continue testing and then report the irregularity to the test administrator after the test. This may be done by asking that the test administrator note the irregularity on the Supervisor's Irregularity Report or you can write to Thomson Prometric, DSST Program, 2000 Lenox Drive, Third Floor, Lawrenceville, NJ 08648, and indicate the form and question number(s) or circumstances as well as your name and address.

When will I receive my score report?

Allow approximately four weeks from the date of testing to receive your score report. Allow six to eight weeks to receive a score report for the *Principles of Public Speaking* examination.

Will my test scores be released without my permission?

Your test score will not be released to anyone other than the school you designate on your answer sheet unless you write to us and ask us to send a transcript elsewhere. Instructions about how to do this can be found on your score report. Your scores may be used for research purposes, but individual scores are never made public nor are individuals identified if research findings are made public.

If I do not achieve a passing score on the test, how long must I wait until I can take the test again?

If you do not receive a score on the test that will enable you to obtain credit for the course, you may take the test again after six months (180 days). Please do not attempt to take the test before six months (180 days) have passed because you will receive a score report marked *invalid* and your test fee will not be refunded.

Can my test scores be canceled?

The test administrator is required to report any irregularities to Thomson Prometric. The consequence of bringing unauthorized materials into the testing room, or giving or receiving help, will be the forfeiture of your test fee and the invalidation of test scores. The DSST Program reserves the right to cancel scores and not issue score reports in such situations.

What can I do if I feel that my test scores were not accurately reported?

Thomson Prometric recognizes the extreme importance of test results to candidates and has a multi-step quality-control procedure to help ensure that reported scores are accurate. If you have reason to believe that your score(s) were not accurately reported, you may request to have your answer sheet reviewed and hand scored.

The fees for this service are:

- $20 fee if requested within six months of the test date
- $30 fee if requested more than six months from the test date
- $30 fee if a re-evaluation of the *Principles of Public Speaking* speech is requested

The fee for this service can be paid by credit card or by certified check or U.S. money order payable to Thomson Prometric. Submit your request for score verification along with the appropriate fee or credit card information (credit card number and expiration date) to Thomson Prometric, DSST Program, 2000 Lenox Drive, Third Floor, Lawrenceville, NJ 08648. Include your full name, the test title, the date you took the test, and your Social Security number. Candidates will be notified if a scoring discrepancy is discovered within four weeks of receipt of the request.

What does ACE recommendation mean?

The ACE recommendation is the minimum passing score recommended by the American Council on Education for any given test. It is equivalent to the average score of students in the DSST norming sample who received a grade of C for the course. Some schools require a score higher than the ACE recommendation.

Who is NLC?

National Learning Corporation (NLC) has been successfully preparing candidates for 40 years for over 5,000 exams. NLC publishes Passbook® study guides to help candidates prepare for all DANTES and CLEP exams and almost every other type of exam from high school through adult career.

Go to our website — www.passbooks.com — or call (800) 632-8888 for information about ordering our Passbooks.

To get detailed information on the DSST program and DSST preparation materials, visit www.getcollegecredit.com.

If you are interested in taking the DSST exams, call 877-471-9860 or e-mail pnj-dsst@thomson.com.

Fact Sheet

DANTES Subject Standardized Tests

HUMAN RESOURCE MANAGEMENT

TEST INFORMATION

This test was developed to enable schools to award credit to students for knowledge equivalent to that which is learned by students taking the course. The school may choose to award college credit to the student based on the achievement of a passing score. The passing score for each examination is determined by the school based on recommendations from the American Council on Education (ACE). This minimum credit-awarding score is equal to the mean score of students in the norming sample who received a grade of C in the course. Some schools set their own standards for awarding credit and may require a higher score than the ACE recommendation. Students should obtain this information from the institution where they expect to receive credit.

CONTENT

The following topics, which are commonly taught in courses on this subject, are covered by this examination.

	Approximate Percent
I. An Overview of the Human Resource Management Field	4%
A. Historical development B. Human resource functions C. The human resource manager D. Motivation, communication, and leadership E. Ethical aspects of human resource decision making	
II. Human Resource Planning	6%
A. Strategic human resource issues B. Job analysis and job design	
III. Staffing	15%
A. Recruiting B. Selection C. Promotions and transfers D. Reduction-in-force E. Voluntary turnover	
IV. Training and Development	11%
A. Orientation B. Career planning C. Principles of learning D. Training programs and methods E. Development programs	
V. Performance Appraisals	10%
A. Reasons for performance evaluation B. Techniques C. Problems	
VI. Compensation Issues	15%
A. Job evaluation B. Wage and salary administration C. Compensation systems D. Benefits - mandatory and voluntary	
VII. Safety and Health	5%
A. Occupational accidents and illness B. Quality of work life C. Workplace security	
VIII. Employee Rights and Discipline	5%

from the official announcement for instructional purposes

A subsidiary of

	Approximate Percent
IX. Employment Law	**15%**

A. Equal employment opportunity laws (e.g., Civil Rights Act Title VII, ADA, ADEA)
B. Compensation and benefits related laws (e.g., ERISA, FMLA, FLSA)
C. Health, safety and employee rights laws (e.g., OSHA, WARN)
D. Union laws (e.g., NLRA, Taft-Hartley Act, Civil Service Reform Act)

X. Labor Relations	**6%**

A. Unions
B. Collective bargaining
C. Unionized versus non-unionized work settings

XI. International Human Resource Management	**4%**
XII. Current Issues and Trends	**4%**

A. Workforce diversity
B. Human resource information systems
C. Changing patterns of work relationships (e.g., virtual office, contingent workers, autonomous work groups)

Questions on the test require candidates to demonstrate the following abilities. Some questions may require more than one of the abilities.

- Knowledge of basic facts and terms
  (about 35-40% of the examination)
- Understanding of concepts and principles
  (about 30-35% of the examination)
- Ability to apply knowledge to specific problems and situations
  (about 25-30% of the examination)

SAMPLE QUESTIONS

1. Specific standardized questions are used primarily in which of the following types of interviews?

   (A) Patterned or structured
   (B) Nondirective
   (C) Group or board
   (D) Stress

2. Organizational or companywide incentive plans include all of the following EXCEPT

   (A) employee stock ownership plans (ESOP's)
   (B) Scanlon plans
   (C) profit-sharing plans
   (D) standard-hour plans

3. Which of the following theories of employee motivation distinguishes between "satisfiers" and "dissatisfiers"?

   (A) Herzberg's Maintenance Theory
   (B) Maslow's Need Hierarchy
   (C) McClelland's Achievement Theory
   (D) McGregor's Theory X and Theory Y

4. A full-time employee of a local union is generally known as a
   (A) shop steward
   (B) national representative
   (C) business agent
   (D) union organizer

5. Which of the following programs frequently uses simulation to train employees?

   (A) Apprenticeship training
   (B) On-the-job training
   (C) Job instruction training
   (D) Vestibule training

6. Which of the following statements is NOT true about exempt employees?

   (A) They are subject to the overtime provisions of the Fair Labor Standards Act.
   (B) They are permitted to bargain collectively under the provisions of the Tart-Hartley Act.
   (C) They are permitted to have flexible work schedules.
   (D) They are paid hourly wage rates.

7. A job specification is usually a written document that

   (A) specifies how a job is to be done
   (B) outlines the specific duties of a job
   (C) lists the employee characteristics required to perform a job
   (D) describes the process used to obtain specific job information

8. Which of the following performance appraisal methods does NOT require the supervisor to compare the performances of subordinate employees in the unit?

   (A) The forced-choice method
   (B) The forced-distribution method
   (C) The paired-comparison method
   (D) The ranking method

9. The Hay Plan is best known as

   (A) an incentive plan
   (B) a job evaluation plan
   (C) a pension plan
   (D) a performance evaluation plan

STUDYING FOR THE EXAMINATION

The following is a list of reference publications that were being used as textbooks in college courses of the same or similar title at the time the test was developed. Appropriate textbooks for study are not limited to those listed below. If you wish to obtain study resources to prepare for the examination, you may reference either the current edition of the following titles **or** textbooks currently used at a local college or university for the same class title. It is recommended that you reference **more than one textbook** on the topics outlined in this fact sheet. You should **begin by checking textbook content against the content outline** included on the front page of this Fact Sheet **before** selecting textbooks that cover the test content from which to study. Textbooks may be found at the campus bookstore of a local college or university offering a course on the subject.

Sources for study material suggested but not limited to the following:

Carrell, Michael R., Frank D. Kuzmits, and Norbert S. Elbert. *Personnel: Human Resource Management.* Columbus, OH: Charles E. Merrill Publishing Co., current edition.

Cascio, Wayne F. *Managing Human Resources.* New York: McGraw-Hill, current edition.

French, Wendell L. *Human Resource Management.* Boston: Houghton Mifflin, current edition.

Heneman, Herbert G. et al. *Personnel/Human Resource Management.* Homewood, IL: Richard D. Irwin, Inc., current edition.

Ivancevich, John M., and William F. Gluech. *Foundations of Personnel/Human Resource Management.* Homewood, IL: BPI/Irwin, current edition.

Leap, Terry L., and Michael D. Crino. *Personnel/Human Resource Management.* New York: MacMillan, current edition.

Mathis, Robert L., and John H. Jackson, *Personnel.* Anaheim, CA: West Publishing Co., current edition.

Mondy, R. Wayne, and Robert M. Noe. *Personnel: The Management of Human Resources.* Needham Heights, MA: Allyn and Bacon, current edition.

Schuler, Randall J., and Vandra L. Huber. *Personnel and Human Resource Management.* Anaheim, CA: West Publishing Co., current edition.

Sherman, Arthur H., George W. Bohlander, and Herbert J. Chruden. *Managing Human Resources.* Cincinnati, OH: South-Western Publishing Co., current edition.

Werther, William B., Jr., and Keith Davis. *Human Resource and Personnel Management.* New York: McGraw-Hill, current edition.

Current textbook used by a local college or university for a course on the subject.

CREDIT RECOMMENDATIONS

The Center For Adult Learning and Educational Credentials of the American Council on Education (ACE) has reviewed and evaluated the DSST examination development process. ACE has made the following recommendations:

Area or Course Equivalent:	Human Resource Management
Level:	Lower level baccalaureate
Amount of Credit:	Three (3) semester hours
Source:	ACE Commission on Educational Credit and Credentials

INFORMATION

Colleges and universities that would like to review additional information about the national norming, or assistance in local norming or score validation studies should write to: DSST Program, Mail Stop 11-P, The Chauncey Group International, 664 Rosedale Road, Princeton, New Jersey 08540.

It is advisable that schools develop a consistent policy about awarding credit based on scores from this test and that the policy be reviewed periodically. The Chauncey Group will be happy to help schools in this effort.

Correct Responses to sample questions: 1A; 2D; 3A; 4C; 5D; 6A; 7C; 8A; 9B.

I.N. 390530

HOW TO TAKE A TEST

You have studied long, hard and conscientiously.

With your official admission card in hand, and your heart pounding, you have been admitted to the examination room.

You note that there are several hundred other applicants in the examination room waiting to take the same test.

They all appear to be equally well prepared.

You know that nothing but your best effort will suffice. The "moment of truth" is at hand: you now have to demonstrate objectively, in writing, your knowledge of content and your understanding of subject matter.

You are fighting the most important battle of your life—to pass and/or score high on an examination which will determine your career and provide the economic basis for your livelihood.

What extra, special things should you know and should you do in taking the examination?

BEFORE THE TEST

YOUR PHYSICAL CONDITION IS IMPORTANT

If you are not well, you can't do your best work on tests. If you are half asleep, you can't do your best either. Here are some tips:

1) Get about the same amount of sleep you usually get. Don't stay up all night before the test, either partying or worrying—DON'T DO IT!
2) If you wear glasses, be sure to wear them when you go to take the test. This goes for hearing aids, too.
3) If you have any physical problems that may keep you from doing your best, be sure to tell the person giving the test. If you are sick or in poor health, you really cannot do your best on any test. You can always come back and take the test some other time.

AT THE TEST

EXAMINATION TECHNIQUES

1) Read the general instructions carefully. These are usually printed on the first page of the exam booklet. As a rule, these instructions refer to the timing of the examination; the fact that you should not start work until the signal and must stop work at a signal, etc. If there are any *special* instructions, such as a choice of questions to be answered, make sure that you note this instruction carefully.

2) When you are ready to start work on the examination, that is as soon as the signal has been given, read the instructions to each question booklet, underline any key words or phrases, such as *least*, *best*, *outline*, *describe* and the like. In this way you will tend to answer as requested rather than discover on reviewing your paper that you *listed without describing*, that you selected the *worst* choice rather than the *best* choice, etc.

3) If the examination is of the objective or multiple-choice type – that is, each question will also give a series of possible answers: A, B, C or D, and you are called upon to select the best answer and write the letter next to that answer on your answer paper – it is advisable to start answering each question in turn. There may be anywhere from 50 to 100 such questions in the three or four hours allotted and you can see how much time would be taken if you read through all the questions before beginning to answer any. Furthermore, if you come across a question or group of questions which you know would be difficult to answer, it would undoubtedly affect your handling of all the other questions.

4) If the examination is of the essay type and contains but a few questions, it is a moot point as to whether you should read all the questions before starting to answer any one. Of course, if you are given a choice – say five out of seven and the like – then it is essential to read all the questions so you can eliminate the two which are most difficult. If, however, you are asked to answer all the questions, there may be danger in trying to answer the easiest one first because you may find that you will spend too much time on it. The best technique is to answer the first question, then proceed to the second, etc.

5) Time your answers. Before the exam begins, write down the time it started, then add the time allowed for the examination and write down the time it must be completed, then divide the time available somewhat as follows:
   - If 3-1/2 hours are allowed, that would be 210 minutes. If you have 80 objective-type questions, that would be an average of 2-1/2 minutes per question. Allow yourself no more than 2 minutes per question, or a total of 160 minutes, which will permit about 50 minutes to review.
   - If for the time allotment of 210 minutes there are 7 essay questions to answer, that would average about 30 minutes a question. Give yourself only 25 minutes per question so that you have about 35 minutes to review.

6) The most important instruction is to *read each question* and make sure you know what is wanted. The second most important instruction is to *time yourself properly* so that you answer every question. The third most important instruction is to *answer every question.* Guess if you have to but include something for each question. Remember that you will receive no credit for a blank and will probably receive some credit if you write something in answer to an essay question. If you guess a letter – say "B" for a multiple-choice question – you may have guessed right. If you leave a blank as an answer to a multiple-choice question, the examiners may respect your

feelings but it will not add a point to your score. Some exams may penalize you for wrong answers, so in such cases *only*, you may not want to guess unless you have some basis for your answer.

7) Suggestions
   a. Objective-type questions
      1. Examine the question booklet for proper sequence of pages and questions
      2. Read all instructions carefully
      3. Skip any question which seems too difficult; return to it after all other questions have been answered
      4. Apportion your time properly; do not spend too much time on any single question or group of questions
      5. Note and underline key words – *all, most, fewest, least, best, worst, same, opposite,* etc.
      6. Pay particular attention to negatives
      7. Note unusual option, e.g., unduly long, short, complex, different or similar in content to the body of the question
      8. Observe the use of "hedging" words – *probably, may, most likely,* etc.
      9. Make sure that your answer is put next to the same number as the question
      10. Do not second-guess unless you have good reason to believe the second answer is definitely more correct
      11. Cross out original answer if you decide another answer is more accurate; do not erase until you are ready to hand your paper in
      12. Answer all questions; guess unless instructed otherwise
      13. Leave time for review

   b. Essay questions
      1. Read each question carefully
      2. Determine exactly what is wanted. Underline key words or phrases.
      3. Decide on outline or paragraph answer
      4. Include many different points and elements unless asked to develop any one or two points or elements
      5. Show impartiality by giving pros and cons unless directed to select one side only
      6. Make and write down any assumptions you find necessary to answer the questions
      7. Watch your English, grammar, punctuation and choice of words
      8. Time your answers; don't crowd material

8) Answering the essay question

Most essay questions can be answered by framing the specific response around several key words or ideas. Here are a few such key words or ideas:

M's: manpower, materials, methods, money, management
P's: purpose, program, policy, plan, procedure, practice, problems, pitfalls, personnel, public relations

a. Six basic steps in handling problems:
   1. Preliminary plan and background development
   2. Collect information, data and facts
   3. Analyze and interpret information, data and facts
   4. Analyze and develop solutions as well as make recommendations
   5. Prepare report and sell recommendations
   6. Install recommendations and follow up effectiveness

b. Pitfalls to avoid
   1. *Taking things for granted* – A statement of the situation does not necessarily imply that each of the elements is necessarily true; for example, a complaint may be invalid and biased so that all that can be taken for granted is that a complaint has been registered
   2. *Considering only one side of a situation* – Wherever possible, indicate several alternatives and then point out the reasons you selected the best one
   3. *Failing to indicate follow up* – Whenever your answer indicates action on your part, make certain that you will take proper follow-up action to see how successful your recommendations, procedures or actions turn out to be
   4. *Taking too long in answering any single question* – Remember to time your answers properly

EXAMINATION SECTION

EXAMINATION SECTION
TEST 1

DIRECTIONS: Each question or incomplete statement is followed by several suggested answers or completions. Select the one that BEST answers the question or completes the statement. *PRINT THE LETTER OF THE CORRECT ANSWER IN THE SPACE AT THE RIGHT.*

1. According to most research, which of the following factors is generally considered by people as MOST important in deciding to take a job? 1.___
   A. Control of work schedule
   B. Salary/wage
   C. Effect on family or personal life
   D. Employer size

2. The first explicitly *pro-union* federal law passed in the United States was the 2.___
   A. Sherman Antitrust Act of 1890
   B. Clayton Act of 1914
   C. Norris-LaGuardia Act of 1932
   D. Wagner Act of 1935

3. _____ is the system condensing rate ranges into wider classifications for employee rating. 3.___
   A. Broadbanding B. Codetermination
   C. Anchoring D. Dilation

4. During an employment interview, which of the following items of information can be lawfully solicited from an applicant for the purpose of disqualification? 4.___
   A. Arrest record
   B. Prior marital status
   C. Military discharge status, if not the result of a military conviction
   D. Whether candidate has ever worked under a different name

5. Which of the following best describes the effect of the Industrial Revolution (late 18th century) on the field of human resources management? 5.___
   A. The proliferation of mid-level managers
   B. An increasing gap between workers and business owners
   C. A shorter workday for both management and labor
   D. More dangerous working conditions

6. The _____ shop is a practice in which management tries to avoid the organization of labor into a union, without violating labor laws. 6.___
   A. open B. agency C. restricted D. preferential

7. In the field of human resources, the term *central tendency* refers to the
   A. inclination for all workers to perform at an average level
   B. most likely behavior from a group of employees in a given situation
   C. inclination for an employee to remain in a static state, with no desire for advancement
   D. rating of all or most of the employees in the middle of a performance scale

7.___

8. Of all the possible uses for performance evaluations within an organization, which tends to be most INFREQUENTLY used?
   A. Helping organization to identify individual employees' strengths and weaknesses
   B. Wage and salary administration
   C. Promoting communication between superiors and subordinates
   D. Performance feedback

8.___

9. The main obstacle that top management encounters in making strategic planning decisions regarding human resources is that
   A. workers increasingly demand to be included in the process
   B. all other resources are evaluated in terms of money, and in most organizations people are not
   C. human resources are not as important in capital-intensive organizations
   D. in some sectors, turnover rates are too high to allow accurate projections

9.___

10. In what year was the Occupational Safety and Health Administration (OSHA) formed?
    A. 1935 B. 1955 C. 1971 D. 1980

10.___

11. A(n) _____ test will measure how well an applicant can do a sample of work that is to be performed.
    A. proficiency B. aptitude
    C. psychomotor D. job knowledge

11.___

12. Which of the following groups is least likely to benefit from an organization's affirmative action program?
    A. Ethnic minorities B. Religious minorities
    C. Women D. Racial minorities

12.___

13. Which of the following statements about human resources management is LEAST supported by research and field experience?
    A. Human resources management should focus on quality, customer service, employee involvement, productivity, teamwork, and creating a flexible workforce.

13.___

B. The biggest challenge for human resource managers is to shift their attention from current operations to developing strategies for the future.
C. Human resource management practices and policies should be left to human resource managers, so that operating managers can focus on other elements of organizational success.
D. Globalization, downsizing, and the changing demographics of the workforce are the external forces most likely to affect a company's competitiveness in the 21st century.

14. Each of the following is a commonly accepted function of the collective bargaining process, EXCEPT 14.___
A. establishing a method for the settlement of disputes during the lifetime of a contract
B. administering labor agreements
C. determining the appropriate collective bargaining units among groups of workers
D. establishing and revising the rules of the workplace

15. The degree to which a test, interview, or performance evaluation measures skills, knowledge, or an employee's ability to perform is known as _____ validity. 15.___
A. criterion-related B. construct
C. skills D. content

16. Which of the following items of legislation is designed to ensure that handicapped people are not refused a job merely because of their handicap if the handicap does not affect their ability to do a job? 16.___
A. Civil Rights Act of 1964
B. Rehabilitation Act
C. Americans with Disabilities Act
D. Civil Rights Act of 1991

17. Key or benchmark jobs used in pay surveys have each of the following characteristics EXCEPT 17.___
A. they are free of discriminatory employment patterns
B. they are subject to recent shortages or surpluses in the marketplace
C. the work content is relatively stable over time
D. a large number of employees hold them

18. In the human resource planning process, the first step taken is usually 18.___
A. human resource supply analysis
B. forecasting human resource demands
C. action plan development
D. situation analysis

19. In a typical workplace safety management program, the first step taken is typically to 19.___
A. develop effective reporting systems
B. reward supervisors for effective management of the safety function

C. establish indicator systems such as accident statistics
D. develop rules and procedures

20. Which of the following is NOT a power of the Equal Employment Opportunity Commission? To 20.___
A. require employers to report employment statistics
B. bring lawsuits against employers in the federal courts
C. issue directly enforceable orders
D. mediate an agreement between parties when a discrimination complaint is found justified

21. The most common job evaluation method used to determine pay structures within organizations is 21.___
A. the point method
B. classification
C. factor comparison
D. ranking

22. Which of the following items of federal legislation established a minimum wage for specified types of workers? 22.___
A. Civil Rights Act of 1964
B. Railway Labor Act
C. Fair Labor Standards Act
D. Occupational Health and Safety Act

23. Which of the following performance evaluation methods tends to be LEAST useful for the purpose of making promotion decisions? 23.___
A. Behaviorally anchored rating system (BARS)
B. Essay evaluations
C. Critical incident
D. Field review

24. During the planning process for a project, the phase occurs after the objective has been set, in which the supervisor must decide how the objective can be achieved, is typically referred to as the _____ phase. 24.___
A. discussion
B. questioning
C. action planning
D. preplanning

25. According to the EEC's definitions, sexual advances, requests for sexual favors, and other verbal or physical conduct of a sexual nature are considered sexual harassment under each of the following conditions EXCEPT 25.___
A. submission to such conduct is, either explicitly or implicitly, a term or condition of a person's employment
B. submission to or rejection of such conduct is used as the basis for employment decisions affecting the individual
C. the advances or requests are unwelcome
D. such conduct unreasonably interferes with an individual's work or creates a hostile or offensive work environment

KEY (CORRECT ANSWERS)

1. C
2. C
3. A
4. D
5. B

6. C
7. D
8. C
9. B
10. C

11. A
12. B
13. C
14. C
15. D

16. B
17. B
18. D
19. C
20. C

21. A
22. C
23. B
24. C
25. C

TEST 2

DIRECTIONS: Each question or incomplete statement is followed by several suggested answers or completions. Select the one that BEST answers the question or completes the statement. *PRINT THE LETTER OF THE CORRECT ANSWER IN THE SPACE AT THE RIGHT.*

1. Which of the following conditions within an organization is LEAST favorable for implementing a gainsharing plan? 1.___
   A. Product costs are controllable by employees.
   B. The organization is fairly large, usually more than 500 employees.
   C. There is no labor union.
   D. There are few product changes.

2. The most widely used method for training employees is 2.___
   A. vestibule training
   B. computer-assisted instruction
   C. on-the-job training
   D. programmed instruction

3. In human resources management, the term *financial core* refers to 3.___
   A. the secure, low-return investments that stabilize an employee benefit plan
   B. the group of employees whose performance most directly impacts a company's earnings
   C. a company's primary product or service line
   D. members of a union who pay dues but choose not to engage in any other union-related activity

4. In the human resources planning process, which of the following activities is typically performed by the operating manager with input from the human resources manager? 4.___
   A. Analysis of personnel supply
   B. Strategic management decisions
   C. Forecasting personnel demands
   D. Job analysis

5. Title VII of the Civil Rights Act of 1964, as amended, prohibits discrimination based on race, color, religion, sex, or national origin in any term, condition, or privilege of employment. Each of the following types of organizations is subject to the provisions of this legislation EXCEPT 5.___
   A. all public and private educational institutions
   B. private employers of 15 or fewer people
   C. joint labor-management committees for apprenticeships and training
   D. all state and local governments

6. Job _____ is the term for a written explanation of the knowledge, skills, abilities, and other characteristics necessary for effective job performance. 6.___
   A. evaluation
   B. specification
   C. description
   D. analysis

7. In the performance evaluation process, which of the following functions is typically undertaken by the human resource manager and engineers, subject to the approval of an operating manager? 7.___
   A. Filing the performance evaluation
   B. Discussing the evaluation with the employee
   C. Establishing performance standards
   D. Reviewing employee performance

8. The purpose of a pay policy line is to 8.___
   A. summarize the pay rates of various jobs in the labor market
   B. represent an organization's pay level policy relative to what competition pays for similar jobs
   C. document compliance with the Equal Pay Act
   D. determine the minimum total payroll needed to maintain profit and productivity

9. Which of the following recruitment practices is least likely to be reviewed by a government agency for the purpose of determining possible discrimination? 9.___
   A. Estimates of the firm's employment needs for the coming year
   B. Statistics on the number of applicants processed by category
   C. Division of responsibilities between operating managers and human resource managers
   D. Recruiting advertising

10. Another name for *quality circles* in personnel is 10.___
   A. continuous improvement teams
   B. groupthink
   C. formal work groups
   D. functional departments

11. Before implementing an employee training program, an organization often conducts a needs assessment first. Which of the following techniques involves the greatest potential participant involvement in the process? 11.___
   A. Evaluation of past programs
   B. Attitude surveys
   C. Critical incident method
   D. Performance documents

12. In the vocabulary of job analysis, what is the term for a group of positions that are similar in their duties? 12.___
   A. Vocation
   B. Task
   C. Field
   D. Job

13. When assessing the costs and benefits of their training and development programs, many firms rely on the consensus accounting model. According to this model, the final step in this process is 13.___
    A. determining all training cost categories
    B. coding training costs
    C. establishing an organization-specific definition of training
    D. calculating training costs

14. Equal _____ is NOT a factor used to define equal work under the terms of the Equal Pay Act. 14.___
    A. working conditions B. effort
    C. training D. skills

15. Typically, which of the following procedures in the employee selection process is conducted FIRST? 15.___
    A. Interview by human resources department
    B. Employment tests
    C. Interview by supervisor
    D. Background and reference checks

16. Which of the following is an individual performance assessment method? 16.___
    A. Forced distribution B. Paired comparison
    C. Ranking D. Forced choice

17. When a manager evaluates employees' performance by placing a certain percentage of personnel at various performance levels, the method of _____ is being used. 17.___
    A. forced-choice rating
    B. forced-distribution ranking
    C. alteration ranking
    D. central tendency

18. Though a *closed shop* organization is illegal under federal law, many modified closed shops still exist in U.S. labor. Which of the following industries is LEAST likely to operate such an organization? 18.___
    A. Maritime B. Agriculture
    C. Printing D. Construction

19. *Reliability* in personnel selection refers to how stable or repeatable a measurement is over a variety of testing conditions. Which of the following types of reliability is determined by correlating scores from two different configurations of the same selection test? 19.___
    A. Interrater B. Alternate-form
    C. Criterion-related D. Test-retest

20. In the overall union structure, intermediate union bodes are typically responsible for each of the following EXCEPT 20.___
    A. collecting dues from individual members
    B. helping to coordinate union membership

C. joining local unions with similar goals
D. organizing discussion of issues pertaining to labor-management relationships

21. Historically, the big push in the United States for increasing employee benefits occurred during _____, when there was a shortage of work and wages were controlled by the federal government. 21.___
A. the recession of 1890
B. the Great Depression
C. World War II
D. the 1960s

22. An assessment center is a multiple-selection method for obtaining personnel. Which of the following statements about assessment centers is generally FALSE? 22.___
A. Assessors doing the evaluation are usually a panel of line managers from the organization.
B. The centers are used mostly for selecting managers.
C. The centers make extensive use of written tests as well as performance evaluations.
D. All evaluations of applicants are performed on an individual basis.

23. The first step in the collective bargaining process is typically 23.___
A. fact-finding
B. conciliation
C. negotiation
D. concession

24. To an employee, the MAIN advantage of a flexible spending account benefit is that 24.___
A. different employees can be given different minimum spending levels, based on their needs
B. bills are paid with before-tax dollars
C. they provide extensive major medical coverage
D. money left in the account at the end of the year rolls over into the next

25. For which of the following purposes should performance evaluations be based on actual performance rather than potential performance? 25.___
I. Promotion consideration
II. Salary and wage adjustment
III. Improvement of performance

The CORRECT answer is:
A. I *only*
B. I, II
C. II, III
D. I, II, III

KEY (CORRECT ANSWERS)

1. B	6. B	11. C	16. D	21. C
2. C	7. C	12. D	17. B	22. D
3. D	8. B	13. B	18. B	23. B
4. B	9. C	14. C	19. B	24. B
5. B	10. A	15. A	20. A	25. C

EXAMINATION SECTION
TEST 1

DIRECTIONS: Each question or incomplete statement is followed by several suggested answers or completions. Select the one that BEST answers the question or completes the statement. *PRINT THE LETTER OF THE CORRECT ANSWER IN THE SPACE AT THE RIGHT.*

1. An individual incentive plan where pay fluctuates based on units of production per time period is described as 1.___
   A. red circle B. standard-hour
   C. differential piece rate D. straight piecework

2. In the experience of most employees, which of the following career stages lasts approximately from age 30 to 45? 2.___
   A. Midcareer crisis B. Advancement
   C. Maintenance D. Establishment

3. Which of the following statements about effective leadership is generally NOT accepted by human resource managers? 3.___
   A. Employees often expect a supervisor to structure their behavior.
   B. A combination of high-supportive and high-directive styles is often a successful leadership style.
   C. Higher management will often set preferences regarding the leadership styles of lower-level managers and supervisors.
   D. Under emergency or high-pressure situations, emphasis on personal well-being is desirable and often preferred by employees.

4. The Employment Retirement Income Security Act (ERISA), as amended, limits the eligibility requirements that an employer may establish for receiving retirement benefits. Specifically, an employer is prohibited from establishing a requirement of more than _____ of service. 4.___
   A. six months B. one year
   C. 3 years D. 5 years

5. In a company's compensation policy, the most significant factor determining the company's external competitiveness is/are its 5.___
   A. benefits
   B. mix of various forms of pay
   C. career opportunities
   D. level of pay

6. In an organization with a human resources department, which of the following information is most likely to be covered by the human resources manager in orienting a new employee? 6.___

A. Introducing the new employee to other employees in the work unit
B. Communicating the objectives and philosophy of the organization
C. Discussing policies on performance and conduct
D. Familiarizing the employee with the physical work environment

7. The Age Discrimination in Employment Act of 1968 prohibits discrimination against individuals who are over _____ years of age. 7.____
A. 30 B. 40 C. 50 D. 60

8. Which of the following types of personnel are most likely to be recruited with the assistance of private employment agencies? 8.____
A. Commissioned sales B. Office/clerical
C. Production/service D. Managers/supervisors

9. Advocates of hierarchical pay structures believe 9.____
A. equal treatment will result in more knowledgeable employees going unrewarded and unrecognized
B. all employees in an organization have an equal number of compensable factors
C. managers should by virtue of their position earn more than line workers
D. seniority should be the primary factor on which pay is based

10. In designing a training program for employees, it is important to remember that usually the first stage of learning is described as 10.____
A. behavioral B. cognitive
C. performance alteration D. experimental

11. In a(n) _____ situation, all employees pay union dues whether or not they are union members. 11.____
A. decertified B. agency shop
C. craft union D. collective bargaining

12. In the employee training process, which of the following tasks is most likely to be jointly undertaken by both the human resources manager and the operating manager? 12.____
A. Selecting the trainer
B. Developing training criteria
C. Doing the training
D. Evaluating the training

13. In behavioral theory, a decline in the rate of a behavior that is brought about by nonreinforcement is known as 13.____
A. extinction B. norming
C. regression D. conformity

14. Of all the relationships between performance evaluation and other personnel management activities, the most critical to understand today is the relationship between evaluation and
    A. human resources research
    B. equal employment opportunity
    C. motivation
    D. productivity

14.___

15. The main disadvantage of the *hot stove* method of employee discipline is that
    A. its benefits are more long-term than immediate
    B. it fails to recognize individual and situational differences
    C. it invites personal bias on the part of the manager
    D. does not allow for detailed recordkeeping

15.___

16. Today, the average employer can be expected to pay about _____ a year or more per employee for benefits.
    A. $1,000 B. $5,000 C. $9,000 D. $12,000

16.___

17. Supervised training and testing for a minimum time period, until an employee has acquired a minimum skill level, is commonly referred to as
    A. apprenticeship training
    B. vestibule training
    C. on-the-job training
    D. programmed instruction

17.___

18. Most human resource professionals believe that the most effective approach to on-the-job training for managers involves
    A. a mix of transfers (to new geographic locations) and rotations through jobs
    B. mentoring
    C. vestibule training
    D. coaching and counseling, coupled with a structured rotation through jobs and functions

18.___

19. The motivation-maintenance theory of employee management deals primarily with motivation through
    A. job design
    B. collegiality
    C. behavioral modification
    D. external rewards

19.___

20. In what year did the American Federation of Labor (AFL) merge with the Congress of Industrial Organizations (CIO)?
    A. 1886 B. 1938 C. 1955 D. 1966

20.___

21. Which of the following is a *critical-incident* system for rating employees?
    A. Alteration ranking
    B. Behavioral observation scale (BOS)
    C. Classification
    D. Forced-choice rating

21.___

22. Likely pitfalls to management by objectives (MBO) include each of the following EXCEPT 22.___
   A. too much emphasis on the long term
   B. failure to tie MBO results with rewards
   C. too much paperwork
   D. setting too many objectives

23. Typically, organizations that implement group incentive programs are most likely to use _____ as the basis for group pay. 23.___
   A. customer satisfaction
   B. quality
   C. financial measures
   D. productivity measures (output to input ratios)

24. Which of the following skills is most likely to be taught in training programs at a U.S. organization? 24.___
   A. Computer skills
   B. Clerical skills
   C. Executive development
   D. Customer relations

25. If an employer is found guilty, upon inspection by OSHA, of a serious violation of the federal health and safety code, and it is found that the violation is negligent rather than willful, the penalty is typically 25.___
   A. $1,000 per citation
   B. $10,000 per citation
   C. $10,000 or up to six months in jail
   D. $10,000 and/or six months in jail

KEY (CORRECT ANSWERS)

1. D
2. B
3. D
4. B
5. D

6. B
7. B
8. D
9. A
10. B

11. B
12. A
13. A
14. B
15. B

16. C
17. A
18. D
19. A
20. C

21. B
22. A
23. C
24. A
25. A

TEST 2

DIRECTIONS: Each question or incomplete statement is followed by several suggested answers or completions. Select the one that BEST answers the question or completes the statement. *PRINT THE LETTER OF THE CORRECT ANSWER IN THE SPACE AT THE RIGHT.*

1. Which of the following statements about employment agencies and executive search firms is/are TRUE? 1.___
   I. Most employment agencies work on retainer.
   II. Executive agencies are paid only when they have actually provided a new hire.
   III. Executive search firms generally do a better job of maintaining confidentiality.

   The CORRECT answer is:
   A. I *only* B. I, II C. III *only* D. I, II, III

2. _____ is a training method in which, after material is presented in text form, a trainee is required to read and answer questions relating to the text. 2.___
   A. Cross-training B. Programmed instruction
   C. Apprenticeship training D. Classroom training

3. In the training process, which of the following is most likely to be done by the operating manager? 3.___
   A. Doing the training
   B. Developing training criteria
   C. Determining training needs and objectives
   D. Developing training material

4. The purpose of a market pay line is to 4.___
   A. pull the wages of competitors upward
   B. determine the maximum total payroll needed to maintain profit and productivity
   C. discourage the formation of a labor union
   D. summarize the pay rates of various jobs in the labor market

5. When selection procedures at an organization involve the use of tests to measure leadership characteristics and/or personality, tests with _____ validity are generally most appropriate. 5.___
   A. construct B. content
   C. alternate-form D. criterion-related

6. Which of the following is NOT a typical disadvantage associated with variable pay plans? 6.___
   Employees
   A. are unable to minimize risk through diversification
   B. may be likely to intentionally decrease their individual effort

C. tend to count on bonus pay regardless of the likelihood of receiving it
D. may feel penalized for factors beyond their control

7. Which of the following is an employee rating method, using 6 to 10 performance dimensions, that uses critical incidents as anchor statements placed along a scale? 7.___
A. Forced-choice rating
B. Behaviorally anchored rating scale (BARS)
C. Forced-distribution rating
D. Behavioral observation scale (BOS)

8. Many organizations today provide an alternative to traditional career pathing, and base career paths on real-world experiences and individualized preferences. Paths of this kind typically have each of the following characteristics EXCEPT 8.___
A. they are definite and remain stable when organizational needs change
B. they include lateral and downward possibilities
C. each job along the path is specified in terms of acquirable skills and knowledge rather than merely educational credentials or work experience
D. they are flexible enough to take individual qualities into account

9. Title VI of the 1964 Civil Rights Act prohibits discrimination based on several characteristics in all programs or activities that receive federal financial aid in order to provide employment. Which of the following types of discrimination is NOT explicitly outlawed by this law? 9.___
A. Race
B. Sex
C. Color
D. National origin

10. Which of the following types of organizations is exempt from the provisions of the Occupational Safety and Health Act? 10.___
A. Businesses employing 15 or fewer people
B. Government contractors for projects whose costs total less than $50,000
C. Businesses employing only family members
D. Businesses in non-industrial service sectors

11. Which of the following is not a legally mandated employee benefit? 11.___
A. Family leave
B. Unemployment compensation
C. Worker's compensation
D. Child care

12. Human resource planning is LEAST likely to be important if the goals of top management include 12.___
A. rapid expansion
B. merging
C. stable growth
D. diversification

13. _____ is the process of grouping personnel activities into related work units. 13.___
   A. Apportionment
   B. Allotment
   C. Blocking
   D. Departmentation

14. Of the following criteria used in the selection process, which is most potentially troublesome in light of equal employment opportunity laws? 14.___
   A. Personal characteristics
   B. Physical characteristics
   C. Experience/past performance
   D. Formal education

15. Each of the following is generally true of a laissez-faire leader and the group in his or her charge EXCEPT 15.___
   A. decisions are typically made by whoever is willing to make them
   B. morale is low
   C. individuals have little interest in their work
   D. the leader is very conscious of his or her position

16. A work situation in which a union is not present and there is no management effort to keep a union out is known as a(n) _____ shop. 16.___
   A. preferential
   B. open
   C. restricted
   D. closed

17. In a job evaluation that is conducted using the point method, which of the following would typically be performed FIRST? 17.___
   A. Preparing job descriptions
   B. Choosing compensable factors
   C. Establishing factor scales
   D. Conducting job analysis

18. The Pregnancy Discrimination Act requires employers to 18.___
   A. allow up to twelve weeks of leave for birth or adoption
   B. ask job candidates whether they are pregnant
   C. not consider pregnancy to be a disability
   D. treat pregnancy just like any other medical condition with regard to fringe benefits and leave policies

19. An agreement between an employee and management, that, as a condition of employment, the employee will not join a labor union, is known as a _____ contract. 19.___
   A. wildcat
   B. zero-tolerance
   C. yellow-dog
   D. submission

20. Effective human resource departments distinguish between employee training as an ongoing activity and training as a strategic tool for attaining the goals of the organization and the employees. In general, training for specific, measurable impact is characterized by a 20.___

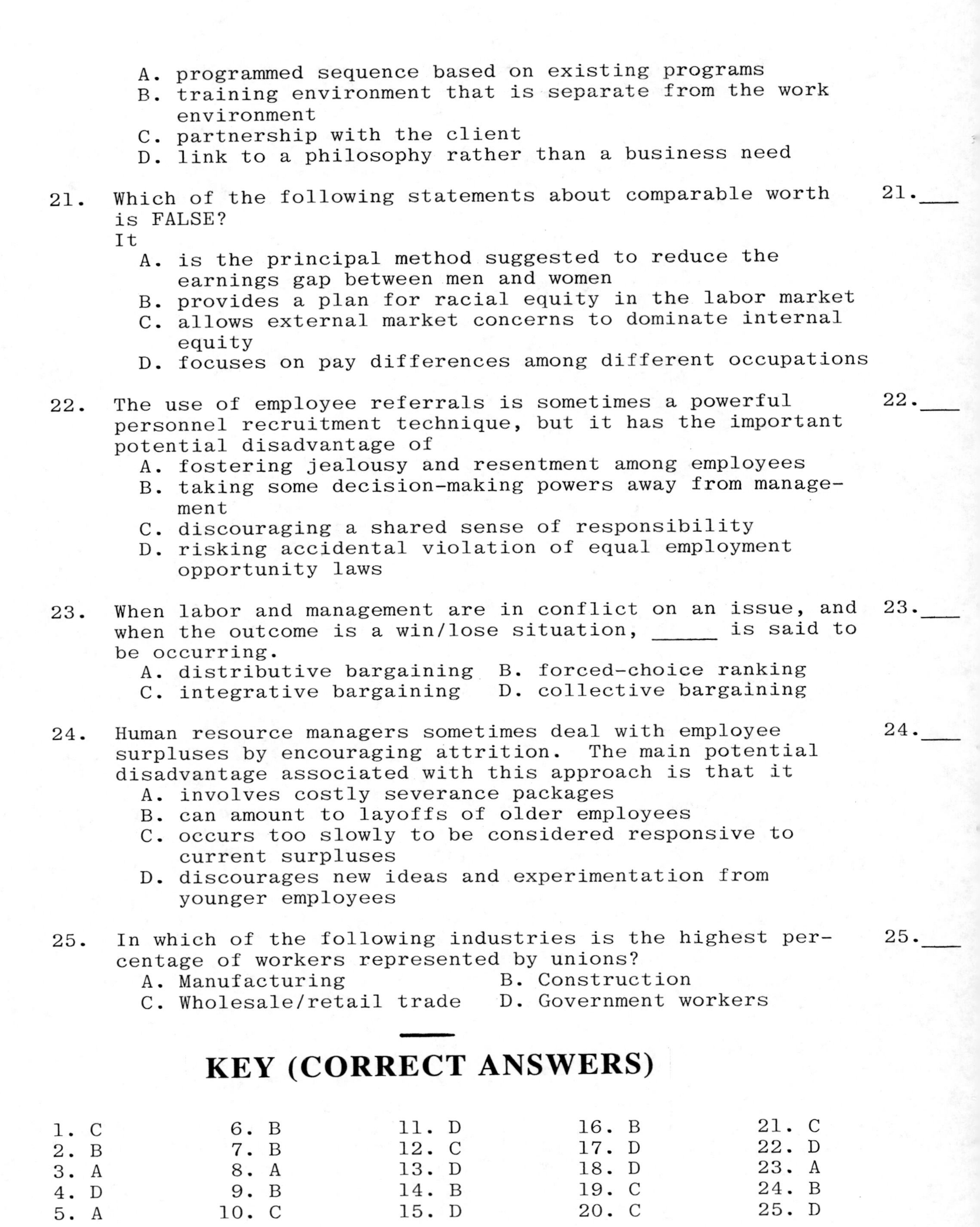

A. programmed sequence based on existing programs
B. training environment that is separate from the work environment
C. partnership with the client
D. link to a philosophy rather than a business need

21. Which of the following statements about comparable worth is FALSE? It 21.___
A. is the principal method suggested to reduce the earnings gap between men and women
B. provides a plan for racial equity in the labor market
C. allows external market concerns to dominate internal equity
D. focuses on pay differences among different occupations

22. The use of employee referrals is sometimes a powerful personnel recruitment technique, but it has the important potential disadvantage of 22.___
A. fostering jealousy and resentment among employees
B. taking some decision-making powers away from management
C. discouraging a shared sense of responsibility
D. risking accidental violation of equal employment opportunity laws

23. When labor and management are in conflict on an issue, and when the outcome is a win/lose situation, _____ is said to be occurring. 23.___
A. distributive bargaining B. forced-choice ranking
C. integrative bargaining D. collective bargaining

24. Human resource managers sometimes deal with employee surpluses by encouraging attrition. The main potential disadvantage associated with this approach is that it 24.___
A. involves costly severance packages
B. can amount to layoffs of older employees
C. occurs too slowly to be considered responsive to current surpluses
D. discourages new ideas and experimentation from younger employees

25. In which of the following industries is the highest percentage of workers represented by unions? 25.___
A. Manufacturing B. Construction
C. Wholesale/retail trade D. Government workers

KEY (CORRECT ANSWERS)

1. C	6. B	11. D	16. B	21. C
2. B	7. B	12. C	17. D	22. D
3. A	8. A	13. D	18. D	23. A
4. D	9. B	14. B	19. C	24. B
5. A	10. C	15. D	20. C	25. D

EXAMINATION SECTION
TEST 1

DIRECTIONS: Each question or incomplete statement is followed by several suggested answers or completions. Select the one that BEST answers the question or completes the statement. *PRINT THE LETTER OF THE CORRECT ANSWER IN THE SPACE AT THE RIGHT.*

1. Which of the following items of federal legislation was designed to encourage the growth of labor unions and restrain management from interfering with that growth? 1.___
   A. Wagner Act
   B. Taft-Hartley Act
   C. Fair Labor Standards Act
   D. Sherman Antitrust Act

2. The _____ training approach to employee training involves a simulation of the real working environment. 2.___
   A. apprenticeship
   B. classroom
   C. vestibule
   D. step

3. Company A is conducting a wage survey in order to determine its external competitiveness. In order to be useful and informative, the survey results must include each of the following EXCEPT 3.___
   A. the names and sizes of the companies surveyed
   B. a brief description of job duties
   C. data from companies that are in the same geographic location
   D. the dates on which listed wages and salaries were in effect

4. In forecasting an organization's demand for employees, which of the following is a *bottom-up* technique? 4.___
   A. Trend projection
   B. Unit demand forecasting
   C. Modeling
   D. Expert estimate

5. What is the term for the method in which a manager continually ranks his or her employees from most valuable to least valuable? 5.___
   A. Object classification
   B. Alteration ranking
   C. Subject categorization
   D. Forced-choice rating

6. In order to be effective, the criteria on which performance evaluations are based should be designed with each of the following in mind EXCEPT 6.___
   A. relevance
   B. practicality
   C. comprehensiveness
   D. sensitivity

7. Historically, the personnel function was considered to be concerned almost exclusively with blue-collar or operating employees, until about the 7.___
   A. 1890s
   B. 1920s
   C. 1960s
   D. 1990s

8. During an employment interview, the solicitation of information about _____, in ANY situation, no matter what the perceived relationship to the job, is unlawful. 8.___
   A. religion
   B. handicaps
   C. race or color
   D. national origin

9. What is the term for the process of unionized employees voting to drop the union? 9.___
   A. Decertification
   B. Opening shop
   C. Exposure
   D. Closing shop

10. All written sexual harassment policies presented by an employer need to contain the following EXCEPT a(n) 10.___
    A. statement encouraging people to come forward with complaints
    B. definition of sexual harassment
    C. alternative channel for filing complaints
    D. promise to make a case public once it has been confirmed and resolved

11. To human resource professionals, the primary advantage associated with computer-aided job evaluations is that they 11.___
    A. decrease the bureaucratic burdens associated with the process
    B. produce results that are more widely accepted
    C. are much more efficient than other kinds of processes
    D. are nearly always less expensive than other methods

12. In order for the National Labor Relations Board to be appropriately petitioned to hold a representation election to determine whether employees in a bargaining unit can be represented by a union, at least _____% of the bargaining unit's employees must sign an authorization card. 12.___
    A. 10 B. 30 C. 50 D. 75

13. Which of the following items of federal legislation was designed to audit and regulate the internal affairs of unions? 13.___
    A. Civil Rights Act of 1964
    B. Landrum-Griffin Act
    C. Fair Labor Standards Act
    D. Robinson-Patman Act

14. Which of the following unions is currently experiencing the most rapid growth rate? 14.___
    A. Service Employees International Union
    B. United Steel Workers
    C. American Federation of Government Employees
    D. United Auto Workers

15. Which of the following is NOT a potential disadvantage associated with a flexible-benefits plan? 15.___
    A. It requires intensive administrative effort.
    B. It often results in erratic cost patterns for the organization.

C. For employees, contributions and deductibles are often increased.
D. It tends to raise the costs of introducing new forms of benefits.

16. Under the Hazard Communications Standard of the Occupational Safety and Health Act, either of the following may complete Material Safety Data Sheets on chemicals imported into, produced, or used in the workplace EXCEPT 16.___
A. employees
B. manufacturers
C. employers
D. importers

17. The term *halo effect* is most often used to refer to cases when a human resources manager 17.___
A. allows a single prominent characteristic of an interviewee to dominate judgment of all other characteristics
B. projects the behaviors and attitudes of one prominent employee onto other employees
C. typifies an employee's work habits by one exceptional example, good or bad
D. considers all of the employees in his or her charge together as one unit, rather than as individuals

18. Approximately how much time should be scheduled by a human resources department to develop a behaviorally anchored rating scale (BARS) for performance evaluation? 18.___
A. 1 working day
B. 2-4 days
C. 2 weeks
D. 6 weeks

19. Each of the following actions, if taken by a human resources manager, is likely to have a positive effect on employee motivation EXCEPT 19.___
A. treating employees as members of a group
B. encouraging participation
C. relating rewards to performance
D. making work interesting

20. Which of the following federal laws prohibited a union to require that a person be a member of a union before he or she is hired? 20.___
A. Sherman Antitrust Act
B. Clayton Act
C. Taft-Hartley Act
D. Landrum-Griffin Act

21. Among the different types of retirement plans, 401(k) plans are classified as 21.___
A. employee stock ownership plans (ESOPs)
B. private pensions
C. tax reduction stock ownership plans (TRASOPs)
D. asset income

22. The strictness of a company's employee discipline policy depends most on 22.___
A. the supportiveness of the work group
B. the nature of the supervisor
C. the nature of the prevailing labor markets
D. existing legal statutes

23. The first union in the United States to achieve significant size and influence was the 23.___
    A. United Garment Workers
    B. American Federation of Labor
    C. Knights of Labor
    D. Congress of Industrial Organizations

24. What is the term for a diagram which vertically represents the activities to be performed, and horizontally represents the time required to perform them? 24.___
    A. Nomograph B. Gantt chart
    C. Layout chart D. Flow-process chart

25. The age discrimination provisions of the Age Discrimination in Employment Act apply to all employers of _____ or more people. 25.___
    A. 5 B. 15 C. 20 D. 100

KEY (CORRECT ANSWERS)

1. A
2. C
3. A
4. B
5. B
6. C
7. C
8. C
9. A
10. A
11. A
12. B
13. B
14. A
15. D
16. A
17. A
18. B
19. A
20. C
21. D
22. C
23. C
24. B
25. C

TEST 2

DIRECTIONS: Each question or incomplete statement is followed by several suggested answers or completions. Select the one that BEST answers the question or completes the statement. *PRINT THE LETTER OF THE CORRECT ANSWER IN THE SPACE AT THE RIGHT.*

1. Which of the following is NOT a disadvantage commonly associated with skill-based pay structures? 1.___
   A. They often result in bloated staffing.
   B. Their compliance with the Equal Pay Act is still undecided on many points.
   C. They are based mostly on job content.
   D. They often become expensive if not properly managed.

2. The number of applicants hired at an organization, divided by the total number of applicants, yields a statistic known as a _____ ratio. 2.___
   A. turnover
   B. market pay
   C. selection
   D. recruitment success

3. Job _____ is the term for the formal process by which the relative worth of various jobs in the organization is determined for pay purposes. 3.___
   A. analysis
   B. specification
   C. evaluation
   D. enlargement

4. Which of the following is NOT an effective means of counteracting commonly-occurring career problems in a new employee? 4.___
   A. Give the employee a challenging initial assignment
   B. De-emphasize a job's negative aspects
   C. Give the employee as much authority as possible
   D. Assign new employees initially to demanding supervisors

5. In the factor comparison method of job evaluation, which of the following is typically performed LAST? 5.___
   A. Benchmark or key jobs are evaluated according to compensable factors.
   B. Key jobs are displayed in a job comparison chart.
   C. Comparison factors are selected and defined.
   D. Evaluators allocate a part of each key job's wage to each job factor.

6. Concerning discipline, employees _____ are usually the easiest to work with and adjust. 6.___
   A. with alcohol- or drug-related problems
   B. whose performance are due to factors directly related to work
   C. whose performance are due to problems caused by the work group
   D. with family problems

7. Among individual performance assessment techniques, the oldest and most commonly used is the 7.___
   A. critical incident technique
   B. forced-choice evaluation
   C. weighted checklist
   D. graphic rating scale

8. The *traditional* theory of human resources management holds that _____ is the primary motivator of people. 8.___
   A. money B. approval
   C. achievement D. safety

9. Generally, under the child labor provisions of the Fair Labor Standards Act, children must be at LEAST _____ years old to be employed in interstate commerce of any kind. 9.___
   A. 12 B. 14 C. 16 D. 18

10. Benefits are typically evaluated by human resource professionals in terms of their objectives. Which of the following objectives tends to be LEAST important in these evaluations? 10.___
    A. Impact on employee families
    B. Fairness or equity with which they are viewed by employees
    C. Cost effectiveness of benefit decisions
    D. Impact on employee work behaviors

11. Which of the following performance assessment techniques tends to involve the highest developmental costs? 11.___
    A. Graphic rating scale
    B. Performance testing
    C. Field review
    D. Management by objectives (MBO)

12. Which of the following types of employees is NOT typically classified as *exempt* under the Fair Labor Standards Act? 12.___
    A. Line workers B. Administrators
    C. Outside sales personnel D. Executives

13. Which of the following is a typical guideline to be followed in the process of orienting a new employee to the workplace? 13.___
    A. The most significant part of orientation deals with necessary job skills and work habits, rather than the nature of the relationship between the new employee and supervisors and/or co-workers.
    B. New employees should be allowed a generous amount of time to adjust to the new workplace before their responsibilities are increased.
    C. New employees should be *sponsored* or directed in the immediate environment by a group of experienced workers.
    D. Orientation should begin with the more general policies of the organization.

14. The _____ theory of employee motivation is based on the assumption that employees are motivated to satisfy a number of needs and that money can satisfy, directly or indirectly, only some of these needs. 14.___
    A. Traditional
    B. Behavioral/reinforcement
    C. Need hierarchy
    D. Achievement-power-affiliation

15. Which of the following is a grouping of a variety of jobs that are similar in terms of work difficulty and responsibility? 15.___
    A. Pay class
    B. Job classification
    C. Broadband
    D. Rate change

16. Which of the following statements is TRUE of recruitment that is performed using realistic job previews (RJPs)? 16.___
    A. RJPs tend to reduce the flow of highly capable applicants into the organization.
    B. RJPs tend to generate an extremely high rate of job offer acceptance.
    C. RJPs make a job look unattractive to some or many applicants.
    D. Employees hired after receiving RJPs tend to have a lower rate of job survival than those using traditional previews.

17. The theory of human behavior based on the belief that people attempt to increase pleasure and decrease displeasure is the _____ theory. 17.___
    A. input-output
    B. achievement-power-affiliation
    C. preference-expectancy
    D. behavioral

18. The agencies most responsible for enforcing equal employment opportunity regulations include each of the following EXCEPT the 18.___
    A. Occupational Health and Safety Administration (OSHA)
    B. Equal Employment Opportunity Commission (EEOC)
    C. federal courts
    D. Office of Federal Contract Compliance Programs (OFCCP)

19. The majority of top-level managers consider _____ as the most important workplace activity for dealing with employee substance abuse. 19.___
    A. employee assistance programs
    B. drug testing
    C. supervisory training programs
    D. drug education programs

20. In the performance evaluation process, which of the following functions is typically undertaken exclusively by the human resource manager, rather than the operating manager? 20.___
   A. Training the raters
   B. Setting the policy on evaluation criteria
   C. Discussing the evaluation with the employee
   D. Choosing the evaluation system

21. Which of the following characteristics is LEAST likely to influence the acceptance of variable pay plans by employees of an organization? 21.___
   A. Ratio of variable pay to base pay (leverage)
   B. Amount of base pay
   C. Risk
   D. Procedural justice

22. Which of the following is a performance simulation test used in the personnel selection process? 22.___
   A. Wonderlic Personnel Test
   B. Wechsler Adult Intelligence Scale
   C. California Test of Mental Maturity
   D. Revised Minnesota Paper Form Board Test

23. The extent to which a technique for selecting employees is successful in predicting important elements of job behavior is known as 23.___
   A. construct validity
   B. job correlation
   C. normative probability
   D. criterion-related validity

24. Critics of the *rotation and transfer* method of on-the-job training for managers argue that this method 24.___
   A. creates generalists who may not be able to manage in many specialized situations
   B. discourages new ideas in the work environment
   C. does not provide authentic work experiences
   D. slows the promotion of highly competent individuals

25. According to the Theory X/Theory Y concept of leadership attitudes, which of the following is a Theory X assumption? 25.___
   A. Commitment to objectives is a function of the rewards associated with their achievement.
   B. The average person learns, under proper conditions, not only to accept but to seek responsibility.
   C. Under the conditions of modern industrial life, the intellectual potentials of the average person are only partially utilized.
   D. The average person prefers to be directed.

KEY (CORRECT ANSWERS)

1. A
2. C
3. C
4. B
5. B

6. B
7. D
8. A
9. C
10. A

11. B
12. A
13. B
14. C
15. A

16. C
17. C
18. A
19. A
20. A

21. B
22. D
23. D
24. A
25. D

EXAMINATION SECTION

TEST 1

DIRECTIONS: Each question or incomplete statement is followed by several suggested answers or completions. Select the one that BEST answers the question or completes the statement. *PRINT THE LETTER OF THE CORRECT ANSWER IN THE SPACE AT THE RIGHT.*

1. Willful violations of OSHA provisions by a corporate employer are punishable by maximum fines of up to _____ upon criminal conviction. 1.___
   A. $5,000 B. $50,000 C. $250,000 D. $500,000

2. Which of the following occurs when employees perceive too narrow a difference between their own pay and that of other colleagues? 2.___
   A. Pay compression B. Wage inflation
   C. Pay survey D. Skills gap

3. A local union typically engages in each of the following activities EXCEPT 3.___
   A. administering contracts B. training union leaders
   C. organizing campaigns D. collecting dues

4. Under existing laws or mandates, affirmative action programs are mandated for the hiring practices of 4.___
   A. public educational institutions
   B. government contractors
   C. federal agencies
   D. all of the above

5. In evaluating a training program, a human resources professional wants specifically to learn whether the knowledge, skills, or abilities learned in training led to an employee's improved performance on the job. Her evaluation of the program would test for _____ validity. 5.___
   A. training B. transfer
   C. intraorganizational D. interorganizational

6. In human resources, *methods study* is concerned with 6.___
   A. the way in which work is distributed among personnel
   B. determining the most efficient way of doing a task or job
   C. determining the minimum number of employees needed to complete a task or job
   D. the criteria used to hire employees

7. Which of the following is/are advantages associated with internal recruiting? 7.___
   I. It offers loyal employees a fair chance at promotion.
   II. It helps protect trade secrets.
   III. It encourages new ideas and competition.

The CORRECT answer is:
A. I *only* B. III *only* C. I, II D. II, III

8. In the vocabulary of job analysis, coordinated and aggregated series of work elements that are used to produce a specific output are referred to as 8.____
A. positions B. jobs C. chores D. tasks

9. During the personnel selection process, human resource professionals sometimes use selection tests that are designed to have what is called *predictive validity*. The primary drawback to using this type of assessment is that 9.____
A. employees are often unwilling to take extensive test batteries
B. an employer must wait until a large enough *predictive* group has been hired to norm the measurement
C. *self-selection* bias can restrict the range of test scores
D. results are often skewed toward applicants with previous experience

10. Jobs whose salaries are below the minimum of the salary range for the job are described as _____ jobs. 10.____
A. broadband B. red circle
C. green circle D. exempt

11. In an organization with a human resources department, which of the following information is most likely to be covered by the operating supervisor in orienting a new employee? 11.____
A. A brief history of the organization
B. Rules, regulations, policies, and procedures
C. Personnel policies
D. Reviewing performance criteria

12. In human resources management, *pay structure* refers to 12.____
A. pay set relative to employees working on different jobs within the organization
B. a grouping of a variety of work jobs that are similar in their difficulty and responsibility requirements
C. pay set relative to employees working on similar jobs in other organizations
D. a survey of the compensation of all employees by all employers in a geographic area, an industry, or an occupational group

13. Which of the following is a provision of the Rehabilitation Act, as amended? 13.____
A. Employers may not cite the potential legal liability for drug-related injuries or accidents as a reason for firing an employee.
B. Employers of 100 or more must establish employee assistance programs (EAPs) for helping drug addicts or alcoholics to recover.

C. Employers of any size may not fire, or refuse to hire, an employee or candidate solely because of alcohol or drug addiction.
D. Drug addiction and alcoholism are not be be considered *disabilities* in the same category as other employee handicaps.

14. A disadvantage of using ranking as a job evaluation method is that 14.___
A. it is the slowest of all job evaluation methods
B. it requires cumbersome descriptions of each job class
C. it is one of the more expensive methods
D. its results are nearly always more subjective than with other methods

15. In an organization that employs at least some union members, union members are sometimes given preferences over nonunion members in areas such as hiring, promotion, and layoff. Preferences given in this situation are often likely to violate the provisions of the _____ Act. 15.___
A. Taft-Hartley B. Wagner
C. Landrum-Griffin D. Fair Labor Standards

16. In human resources management, the _____ principle states that authority flows one link at a time, from the top of the organization to the bottom. 16.___
A. parity B. scalar C. quality D. graduation

17. When an employee training program fails, the most common reason is that 17.___
A. training needs changed after the program had been implemented
B. employees were not motivated
C. there were no on-the-job rewards for behaviors and skills learned in training
D. there were inaccurate training needs analyses

18. In implementing a progressive discipline pattern with a difficult employee, the first step is typically to 18.___
A. issue a written warning to the employee
B. impose a period of *decision leave* for the employee to consider his or her actions
C. enroll the employee in additional training
D. counsel or discuss the problem with the employee

19. The most widely used method of career planning that occurs in organizations is 19.___
A. the planning workshop
B. the extended seminar
C. the self-assessment center
D. counseling by supervisors and human resources staff

20. Under the provisions of the Equal Pay Act, differences in _____ is NOT a justification for paying a man more than a woman for the same job. 20.___
A. performance B. skill
C. family situations D. seniority

21. Compensation plans that protect the wages of workers hired before a certain date but start new workers at a lower pay rate are described as 21.___
A. straight piecework B. weighted
C. two-tiered D. differential piece rate

22. To prevent bias and legal complications, performance evaluations should steer clear of each of the following traits EXCEPT 22.___
A. dependability B. knowledge
C. attitude D. drive

23. The type of benefits most valued by employees are typically 23.___
A. paid vacation and holidays
B. medical
C. long-term disability
D. dental

24. Which of the following is the most common reason for employees to be opposed to the process of performance evaluation? 24.___
A. Interference with normal work patterns
B. Operating problems
C. Bad system design
D. Rater subjectivity

25. _____ training is most commonly used in the workplace. 25.___
A. Apprenticeship B. Vestibule
C. Cross- D. Classroom

KEY (CORRECT ANSWERS)

1. D
2. A
3. B
4. B
5. B

6. B
7. C
8. D
9. B
10. C

11. D
12. A
13. B
14. D
15. A

16. B
17. C
18. D
19. D
20. C

21. C
22. B
23. B
24. D
25. D

TEST 2

DIRECTIONS: Each question or incomplete statement is followed by several suggested answers or completions. Select the one that BEST answers the question or completes the statement. *PRINT THE LETTER OF THE CORRECT ANSWER IN THE SPACE AT THE RIGHT.*

1. In today's personnel market, the most critical factor used by recruiters to evaluate prospective job candidates who hold an MBA is usually the 1.___
   A. institution from which the degree was earned
   B. applicant's interpersonal style
   C. applicant's demonstrated skill level
   D. applicant's previous work experience

2. If a human resources manager decides to implement a preventive health care program in the workplace, he or she should be careful to guard against 2.___
   A. an increase in the number of medical claims made by employees
   B. a lack of quantifiable proof that the program is saving money or increasing productivity
   C. the splintering of the wellness program into its own budgetary status
   D. the abuse of available resources by employees

3. Competition is most likely to be a problem in performance evaluations that involve rating by 3.___
   A. the employee's subordinates
   B. the employee's peers
   C. self-evaluation
   D. a committee of several supervisors

4. Which of the following is not a problem commonly associated with merit pay systems? 4.___
   A. Employees often fail to make the connection between pay and performance.
   B. The size of merit awards has little effect on performance.
   C. Costs are usually higher than in individual incentive plans.
   D. The secrecy of rewards is seen as inequity by employees.

5. Which of the following step in the job analysis process is typically performed FIRST? 5.___
   A. Collecting data
   B. Selecting the jobs to be analyzed
   C. Determining how job analysis information will be used
   D. Preparing job descriptions

6. In which of the following sectors are employees typically most expensive to train? 6.___
   A. Consumer products
   B. Agriculture/forestry/fishing
   C. Services
   D. Industrial products

7. A commonly encountered disadvantage of using Bureau of Labor Statistics (BLS) data in pay surveys is that they 7.___
   A. tend to skew data in a way that favors labor over management
   B. are too generalized to be useful
   C. only list maximum and minimum pay rates, not medians and averages
   D. are not widely available to the public

8. Other than the salaries of training staff and trainees, which of the following is typically the largest expense involved in conducting an employee training program? 8.___
   A. Seminars and conferences
   B. Outside services
   C. Facilities and overhead
   D. Hardware

9. Under the provisions of the Equal Pay Act, differences in pay for equal work are permitted if they result from any of the following EXCEPT differences in 9.___
   A. seniority
   B. quality of performance
   C. age
   D. quantity or quality of production

10. Which of the following personnel selection procedures is typically LEAST costly? 10.___
   A. Background and reference checks
   B. Employment interview
   C. Preliminary screening
   D. Employment tests

11. Which of the following is a strictly internal method of personnel recruitment? 11.___
   A. Employment agencies
   B. Recruitment advertising
   C. Special-events recruiting
   D. Job posting

12. Of the following individual performance evaluation techniques, which has the advantage of offering the flexibility to discuss what the organization is attempting to accomplish? 12.___
   A. Graphic rating scale
   B. Behaviorally anchored rating scale (BARS)
   C. Essay evaluation
   D. Behavioral observation scale (BOS)

13. In human resources management, the *Pygmalion effect* refers to the tendency of an employee to
   A. live up to a manager's expectations
   B. identify with a working group
   C. sacrifice his or her personal life for improved work performance
   D. avoid work if at all possible

13.___

14. In medium-sized and larger organizations, the role of a human resources manager in the selection process is most often characterized by
   A. conducting the selection interview
   B. narrowing a field of applicants to a smaller, more manageable number
   C. designing the process by which candidates will be selected
   D. exercising final authority for hiring decisions

14.___

15. Employees who believe they have been discriminated against under the *whistleblowing* provisions of the Occupational Safety and Health Act may file a complaint at the nearest OSHA office within _____ of the alleged discriminatory action.
   A. 10 days   B. 30 days   C. 90 days   D. 6 months

15.___

16. Of the many applications possible with computerized human resource information systems, which of the following is most commonly used?
   A. Equal employment opportunity records
   B. Job analysis
   C. Performance appraisals
   D. Career pathing

16.___

17. _____ cost(s) is the term for expenditures for necessary items that do not become a part of a product or service.
   A. Operating supplies   B. Overhead
   C. Maintenance   D. Material

17.___

18. The union official who is responsible for representing the interests of local members in their relations with managers on the job is the
   A. president   B. business representative
   C. committee person   D. vice president

18.___

19. Of the many types of employment tests used in personnel selection, _____ tests tend to have the highest validities and reliabilities.
   A. performance simulation
   B. paper-and-pencil
   C. job sample performance
   D. personality and temperament

19.___

20. If an employee exhibits a *behavior discrepancy* -- if his or her performance varies from what is expected on the job -- a human resources manager might conduct a performance analysis. Most of these analyses begin with the process of 20.___
   A. motivating the employee to do better
   B. setting clear standards for performance on the job
   C. training the employee
   D. conducting a cost/value analysis of correcting the identified behavior

21. It is NOT a common goal of the orientation process to 21.___
   A. reduce personnel turnover
   B. reduce anxiety
   C. develop realistic expectations
   D. teach an employee specific job skills

22. In order for a situation to be accurately described as a job *layoff*, each of the following conditions must occur EXCEPT 22.___
   A. there is no work available
   B. the work shortage is sudden and surprising
   C. management expects the no-work situation to be temporary
   D. management intends to recall the employee

23. In a(n) _____ payroll plan, pay is based on two separate piecework rates: one for those who produce below or up to standard, and another for those who produce up to standard. 23.___
   A. equity B. Taylor
   C. functional D. distributive

24. Approximately what percentage of the U.S. labor force is currently unionized? 24.___
   A. 5 B. 15 C. 45 D. 70

25. The _____ principle states that managers should concentrate their efforts on matters that deviate from the normal and let their employees handle routine matters. 25.___
   A. critical-incident B. flow-process
   C. exception D. democratic

KEY (CORRECT ANSWERS)

1. B	6. D	11. D	16. A	21. D
2. B	7. B	12. C	17. A	22. B
3. B	8. C	13. A	18. C	23. B
4. C	9. C	14. B	19. C	24. B
5. C	10. C	15. B	20. D	25. C

EXAMINATION SECTION
TEST 1

DIRECTIONS: Each question or incomplete statement is followed by several suggested answers or completions. Select the one that BEST answers the question or completes the statement. *PRINT THE LETTER OF THE CORRECT ANSWER IN THE SPACE AT THE RIGHT.*

1. Each of the following is currently a common reason for American employees to distrust unions EXCEPT 1.___
   A. the fact that some well-known union leaders have engaged in illegal acts
   B. the belief that unions stand against individualism and free enterprise
   C. they are viewed as an ineffective means of gaining contracts and processing complaints
   D. they are viewed as being dominated by blue-collar workers

2. The main disadvantage to using a structured interview approach during personnel selection is that it 2.___
   A. is usually more stressful for the interviewee
   B. can produce long periods of uncomfortable silence
   C. requires a good deal of training to conduct
   D. is usually very restrictive

3. Of the different strategies that may be implemented to control the costs of employee benefit plans, which of the following is LEAST likely to generate ill will on the part of employees? 3.___
   A. Increased co-payment or deductible
   B. Case management
   C. Preauthorization before covering certain expenses
   D. Requiring second opinions

4. In which of the following sectors is the National Mediation Board responsible for the final determination of appropriate collective bargaining units? 4.___
   A. Railway and airline
   B. Postal
   C. Private
   D. Federal

5. It is NOT a common reason for using a job evaluation plan to 5.___
   A. develop a basis for a merit pay program
   B. define expectations for individuals in specific jobs
   C. identify to employees a hierarchy of pay progression
   D. provide a basis for wage negotiation in collective bargaining

6. Which of the following is an example of a *content valid* test used in the personnel selection process? A(n) 6.___
   A. written skills test for a short-order cook position
   B. unstructured interview for a supervisory position on a shop floor
   C. typing test for a secretarial position
   D. written personality assessment for a middle-management position at a consumer goods firm

7. Which of the following items of federal legislation specifies unfair labor union practices that are not permitted? 7.___
   A. Wagner Act
   B. Taft-Hartley Act
   C. Fair Labor Standards Act
   D. Landrum-Griffin Act

8. The MOST important drawback to implementing individual incentive systems is that they 8.___
   A. add pay increases to base pay
   B. limit the number of *important* tasks
   C. do not measure performance at the individual level
   D. often sabotage the interdependency of employees

9. During the labor organization process, if employees decide they no longer need a union, or when the union fails to negotiate an initial contract within the first _____ period of certification, decertification elections can be held. 9.___
   A. 90-day B. 3-month C. 6-month D. 12-month

10. In the employee training programs of U.S. organizations, which of the following formal delivery methods is most likely to be used? 10.___
   A. Case studies
   B. Noncomputerized self-study
   C. Videotapes
   D. Role playing

11. In human resources management, the _____ principle states that a manager's authority must be equal to his or her responsibility. 11.___
   A. Peter B. exception
   C. leadership D. parity

12. Which of the following management approaches to collective bargaining illustrates the tactic of *Boulwarism*? 12.___
   A. Responding to labor's offer by mirroring the negotiators' style, whether it is hard-line or accommodating
   B. Viewing the opposition as an adversary, yet recognizing that an agreement must be worked out along legal guidelines

C. Presenting an initial offer as a final offer that will not be altered by negotiation
D. Offering compromise, flexibility, and tolerance in order to bring negotiations to a speedy conclusion

13. Which of the following is/are likely to be advantages associated with using job incumbents in the job analysis process? 13.___
I. They are a better source of information about what work is actually being done, rather than what is supposed to be done
II. Increased acceptance of any work changes that might result from the analysis
III. They tend to have a clearer idea of the importance of their work than managers or supervisors

The CORRECT answer is:
A. I *only* B. I, II C. I, III D. II, III

14. The risk of *negative recruitment* is generally highest when the method of _____ is used. 14.___
A. summer internships
B. job posting
C. special-events recruiting
D. college recruiting

15. Which of the following is NOT an element of merit pay? 15.___
A. Increases based on individual performance evaluations
B. Increases based on years of job-related experience
C. Pay ranges designed to reflect differences in performance or experience
D. Merit increase guidelines that translate a specific performance rating and position in the pay range to a percent merit increase

16. In order to perform an unbiased performance evaluation, an evaluator keeps a diary of employee performance. This practice will be most useful in avoiding the common _____ error in assessment. 16.___
A. contrast effect B. halo effect
C. central tendency D. recency of events

17. Which of the following is the most important factor in assessing claims of discrimination under the Civil Rights Act of 1991 and the Americans with Disabilities Act of 1990? 17.___
The
A. company's overall work environment
B. diversity of the company's existing personnel
C. company's method for job analysis
D. size of the company

18. Employees are LEAST likely to accept performance appraisals involving rating by subordinates if the evaluations are used for the purpose of 18.___
   A. determining raises or promotions
   B. motivation
   C. development
   D. validation of selection tools

19. According to the achievement-power-affiliation theory, which of the following characteristics in an organization will have no effect on an employee's need for affiliation? 19.___
   A. Responsibility
   B. Support
   C. Conflict
   D. Reward

20. OSHA regulations state that each occupational injury and illness must be recorded on Form 200 within _____ from the time the employer first learned of the injury or illness. 20.___
   A. 48 hours
   B. 6 working days
   C. 10 days
   D. 30 days

21. _____ authority is used to support and advise line authority. 21.___
   A. Unstructured
   B. Autocratic
   C. Operating
   D. Staff

22. Performance evaluations that are conducted more often than quarterly will probably be most useful to organizations that 22.___
   A. are in relatively unstable environments
   B. are focused on long-term growth
   C. tend to have older employees
   D. rely heavily on sales personnel

23. In formulating a pay structure, the most crucial factor is the 23.___
   A. number of different jobs
   B. numerical ratio between management and labor positions
   C. size of differentials among jobs
   D. pay level of competitors

24. Among the following, the type of performance evaluation most rarely used involves assessment by 24.___
   A. peers
   B. superiors only
   C. subordinates
   D. self-evaluation

25. When a new employee is required to be a union member when hired, a(n) _____ situation exists. 25.___
   A. agency shop
   B. closed shop
   C. certified
   D. union shop

KEY (CORRECT ANSWERS)

1. C
2. D
3. B
4. A
5. B
6. C
7. B
8. D
9. D
10. C
11. D
12. C
13. B
14. A
15. B
16. D
17. C
18. C
19. A
20. B
21. D
22. A
23. C
24. A
25. B

TEST 2

DIRECTIONS: Each question or incomplete statement is followed by several suggested answers or completions. Select the one that BEST answers the question or completes the statement. *PRINT THE LETTER OF THE CORRECT ANSWER IN THE SPACE AT THE RIGHT.*

1. The main difference between replacement planning and succession planning is that 1.____
   A. replacement planning does not take an employee's age into account
   B. succession planning is more broadly applied and integrated
   C. replacement planning is used primarily with non-technical labor positions
   D. succession planning merely specifies individual replacements for specific jobs

2. Under the provisions of the Americans with Disabilities Act, each of the following practices is prohibited EXCEPT 2.____
   A. participating in contractual arrangements that discriminate against the disabled
   B. limiting the advancement opportunities of disabled employees
   C. firing an employee whose disability diminishes or limits performance of a particular job
   D. using tests or job requirements that tend to screen out the disabled

3. In the overall union structure, the roles of a national union typically include each of the following EXCEPT 3.____
   A. establishing the rules and policies under which local unions may be chartered
   B. exercising a degree of control over the collection of dues and the admission of members
   C. providing the local unions with support for organizing campaigns and administering contracts
   D. providing office space and other facilities for local unions

4. Which of the following is TRUE of multi-skilled pay structures? 4.____
   A. They typically involve clerical employees.
   B. When used, they typically involve about 80% of a company's workforce.
   C. They are most common among large facilities (over 500 employees).
   D. Managerial or supervisory employees are almost never included.

5. Which of the following states has in effect *right-to-work* laws that ban any form of compulsory union membership? 5.___
   A. Ohio
   B. California
   C. Texas
   D. New York

6. The Employment Retirement Income Security Act (ERISA) does NOT 6.___
   A. cover multi-employer benefit plans
   B. establish minimum eligibility requirements for existing private pension plans
   C. require an employer to establish a private pension plan
   D. require an employer to disclose to employees the details of a private pension plan

7. In supervising employees, a manager usually keeps a written record of unusual incidents that show both positive and negative actions by an employee. What is the term for such a record? 7.___
   A. Critical-incident appraisal
   B. Exception record
   C. Forced-choice rating
   D. Deviation journal

8. Which of the following methods for forecasting an organization's demand for employees is usually the LEAST mathematically sophisticated? 8.___
   A. Unit demand forecasting
   B. Modeling
   C. Expert estimate
   D. Trend projection

9. Which of the following federal laws established the National Labor Relations Board (NLRB)? 9.___
   A. Norris-LaGuardia Act
   B. Wagner Act
   C. Taft-Hartley Act
   D. Landrum-Griffin Act

10. Which of the following is a legal way for an organization's management to prevent a union from organizing? 10.___
    A. Providing wages and fringe benefits that make union membership unattractive
    B. Dismissing employees who want to unionize
    C. Promising rewards if a union is voted down
    D. None of the above

11. The main advantage associated with flextime scheduling methods is that the need for _____ is minimized. 11.___
    A. maternity leave
    B. personal time off
    C. sick days
    D. family leave

12. Which of the following types of labor strikes is considered illegal because it constitutes an invasion of private property? 12.___
    A. Wildcat
    B. Sitdown
    C. Jurisdictional
    D. Economic

13. If the primary purpose of a performance evaluation method is development, and costs are to be a consideration, which of the following methods is most appropriate? 13.____
  A. Essay evaluation
  B. Management by objectives (MBO)
  C. Behavioral observation scales (BOS)
  D. Paired comparison

14. Currently, the erosion of union power in the U.S. labor market rests on each of the following factors EXCEPT 14.____
  A. a decrease in demand by nonunionized employees for union representation
  B. a shift in the workforce from blue-collar manufacturing workers to better-paid service and knowledge workers
  C. the increasing protections already afforded U.S. laborers by federal labor legislation
  D. increased product market competitiveness in a global market

15. Of all the different kinds of benefits and services that can be offered to employees, the least preferred seem to be 15.____
  A. child care
  B. life insurance
  C. social and recreational programs
  D. educational programs

16. When labor and management are in conflict on a common problem, and when the outcome is a win/win situation, _____ bargaining is said to be occurring. 16.____
  A. distributive B. differential
  C. integrative D. collective

17. According to the provisions of the Civil Rights Act of 1991, a plaintiff who sues an organization for intentional hiring or workplace discrimination is limited to a damages cap of _____ if the organization employs between 100 and 200 people. 17.____
  A. $50,000 B. $100,000 C. $200,000 D. $300,000

18. Which of the following is generally TRUE of an autocratic leader and the group in his or her charge? 18.____
  A. Production is usually low in the leader's absence.
  B. The leader does not set goals for the group.
  C. A feeling of responsibility is developed within the group.
  D. Quality of work is generally high.

19. Which of the following is NOT a typical feature of a programmed instruction training program? 19.____
  A. The learner receives immediate feedback on her progress.
  B. Instruction is provided under the supervision of a human instructor.
  C. Behaviorist learning principles are followed closely.
  D. The learner learns at her own rate.

20. Which of the following groups of employees is most at risk for alcoholism? 20.___
   A. Those aged 20-30 who do not have families
   B. Those aged 25-40 who have made many lateral moves within a single organization
   C. Those aged 35-55 who have been employed at the same enterprise for 14-20 years
   D. Older employees (55-65) nearing retirement who have worked with a company for most of their lives

21. Which of the following performance evaluation methods is most useful for the purpose of counseling and development of employees? 21.___
   A. Paired comparison
   B. Ranking
   C. Graphic rating scale
   D. Management by objectives (MBO)

22. In human resources management, *routing* refers to 22.___
   A. the assignment of tasks to newly hired employees
   B. an employee's promotion through the company hierarchy
   C. determining the best sequence of operations
   D. the elimination of unnecessary or unproductive employees

23. Which of the following needs assessment techniques, conducted prior to implementation of a training program, is the most time-consuming? 23.___
   A. Advisory committees
   B. Group discussion
   C. Assessment centers
   D. Skills testing

24. At a certain school district, a bachelor's degree in education places a teacher at *step one* on the salary scale. An additional nine semester hours of college coursework earns an increase of $400. This is an example of a 24.___
   A. skill-based pay structure
   B. knowledge-based pay structure
   C. pay level determined by internal competitiveness
   D. pay level determined by external competitiveness

25. Which of the following is considered a health hazard rather than a safety hazard? 25.___
   A. Exposure to hazardous chemicals
   B. Unsafe machinery
   C. Biological hazards
   D. Poorly maintained equipment

KEY (CORRECT ANSWERS)

1. B
2. C
3. D
4. D
5. C
6. C
7. A
8. C
9. B
10. A
11. B
12. B
13. A
14. C
15. C
16. C
17. B
18. A
19. B
20. C
21. D
22. C
23. D
24. B
25. C

EXAMINATION SECTION
TEST 1

DIRECTIONS: Each question or incomplete statement is followed by several suggested answers or completions. Select the one that BEST answers the question or completes the statement. *PRINT THE LETTER OF THE CORRECT ANSWER IN THE SPACE AT THE RIGHT.*

1. Competent civil service personnel cannot come just from initial employment on a competitive basis and equal pay for equal work. 1.___
   The one of the following additional factors which is of GREATEST importance in building up a body of competent civil service employees is
   A. analysis of work methods and introduction of streamlined procedures
   B. training for skill improvement and creating a sense of belonging
   C. rotation of employees from organization to organization in order to prevent stagnation
   D. treating personnel problems on a more impersonal basis in order to maintain an objective viewpoint
   E. recruiting for all higher positions from among the body of present employees

2. A comment made by an employee about a training course was: *Half of the group seem to know what the course is about, the rest of us can't keep up with them.* 2.___
   The FUNDAMENTAL error in training methods to which this criticism points is
   A. insufficient student participation
   B. failure to develop a feeling of need or active want for the material being presented
   C. that the training session may be too long
   D. that no attempt may have been made to connect the new material with what was already known by any member of the group
   E. that insufficient provision has been made by the instructor for individual differences

3. The one of the following which is NOT a major purpose of an employee suggestion plan is to 3.___
   A. provide an additional method by means of which an employee's work performance can be evaluated
   B. increase employee interest in the work of the organization
   C. provide an additional channel of communication between the employee and top management
   D. utilize to the greatest extent possible the ideas and proposals of employees
   E. provide a formal method for rewarding the occasional valuable idea

4. The pay plan is a vital aspect of a duties classification. In fact, in most areas of personnel administration, pay plan and classification are synonymous. 4.___
This statement is
   A. *correct* in general; while the two are not, in general, synonymous, the pay plan is such a vital aspect that without it the classification plan is meaningless and useless
   B. *not correct*; while the pay plan is a vital aspect of a classification plan, it is not the only one
   C. *correct* in general; pay plan and duties classification are simply two different aspects of the same problem - *equal pay for equal work*
   D. *not correct*; although classification is usually a vital element of a pay plan, a pay plan is not essential to the preparation of a duties classification
   E. *meaningless* unless the specific nature of the classification plan and the pay plan are set forth

5. The one of the following objectives which is MOST characteristic of intelligent personnel management is the desire to 5.___
   A. obtain competent employees, and having them to provide the climate which will be most conducive to superior performance, proper attitudes, and harmonious adjustments
   B. coordinate the activities of the workers in an organization so that the output will be maximized and cost minimized
   C. reduce the dependence of an organization on the sentiments, ambitions, and idiosyncracies of individual employees and thus advance the overall aims of the organization
   D. recruit employees who can be trained to subordinate their interests to the interests of the organization and to train them to do so
   E. mechanize the procedures involved so that problems of replacement and training are reduced to a minimum

6. An organizational structure which brings together, in a single work unit, work divisions which are non-homogeneous in work, in technology, or in purpose will tend to decrease the danger of friction. 6.___
This opinion is, in general,
   A. *correct*; individious comparisons tend to be made when everyone is doing the same thing
   B. *not correct*; a homogeneous organization tends to develop a strong competitive spirit among its employees
   C. *correct*; work which is non-homogeneous tends to be of greater interest to the employee, resulting in less friction
   D. *not correct*; persons performing the same type of work tend to work together more efficiently
   E. *correct*; the presence of different kinds of work permits better placement of employees, resulting in better morale

7. Of the following, the MOST accurate statement of current theory concerning the ultimate responsibility for employee training is that 7.___
   A. ultimate responsibility for training is best separated from responsibility for production and administration
   B. ultimate responsibility for training should be in the hands of a training specialist in the central personnel agency
   C. a committee of employees selected from the trainees should be given ultimate responsibility for the training program
   D. a departmental training specialist should be assigned ultimate responsibility for employee training
   E. each official should be ultimately responsible for the training of all employees under his direction

8. The BEST of the following ways to reduce the errors in supervisors' ratings of employee performance caused by variations in the application of the rating standards is to 8.___
   A. construct a method for translating each rating into a standard score
   B. inform each supervisor of the distribution of ratings expected in his unit
   C. review and change any rating which does not seem justified by the data presented by the rating supervisor
   D. arrange for practice sessions for supervisors at which rating standards will be applied and discussed
   E. confer with the supervisor when a case of disagreement is discovered between supervisor and review board

9. Which capsule description, among the following, constitutes an optimum arrangement of the hierarchical organization of a large-city central personnel agency? 9.___
   A. Three commissioners who appoint a Director of Personnel to carry out the administrative functions but who handle the quasi-judicial and quasi-legislative duties themselves
   B. A Director of Personnel and two Commissioners all three of whom participate in all aspects of the agency's functions
   C. A Director of Personnel who is responsible for making the final decision in all matters pertaining to personnel administration in a city
   D. A Director of Personnel who is the chief administrator and two Commissioners who, together with the Director, handle the quasi-judicial and quasi-legislative duties
   E. Three Commissioners who have review powers over the acts of the Director of Personnel who is appointed on the basis of a competitive examination

10. The one of the following which is a major objective expected to be gained by setting up a personnel council composed of representatives of the central personnel agency and departmental personnel officers is to 10.___
    A. provide an appeal board to which employees who feel grieved can appeal
    B. allow the departments to participate in making the day-to-day decisions faced by the central personnel agency
    C. prevent the departments from participating in making the day-to-day decisions faced by the central personnel agency
    D. establish good communications between the central personnel agency and the departments
    E. develop a broad base of responsibility for the actions of the central personnel agency

11. The one of the following which should be the starting point in the development of an accident reduction or prevention program is the 11.___
    A. institution of an interorganizational safety contest
    B. improvement of the conditions of work so that accidents are prevented
    C. inauguration of a safety education program to reduce accidents due to carelessness
    D. organization of unit safety committees to bring home the importance of safety to the individual worker
    E. determination of the number, character, and causes of accidents

12. An orientation program for a group of new employees would NOT usually include 12.___
    A. a description of the physical layout of the organization
    B. a statement of the rules pertaining to leave, lateness, overtime, and so forth
    C. detailed instruction on the job each employee is to perform
    D. an explanation of the lines of promotion
    E. a talk on the significance of the role the department plays in the governmental structure

13. The device of temporary assignment of an employee to the duties of the higher position is sometimes used to determine promotability. 13.___
The use of this procedure, especially for top positions, is
    A. *desirable*; no test or series of tests can measure fitness to the same extent as actual trial on the job
    B. *undesirable*; the organization will not have a responsible head during the trial period
    C. *desirable*; employees who are on trial tend to operate with greater efficiency

D. *undesirable*; the organization would tend to deteriorate if no one of the candidates for the position was satisfactory
E. *desirable*; the procedure outlined is simpler and less expensive than any series of tests

14. Frequently, when accumulating data for a salary standardization study, the salaries for certain basic positions are compared with the salaries paid in other agencies, public and private. 14.___
The one of the following which would MOST usually be considered one of these basic positions is
A. Office Manager
B. Administrative Assistant
C. Chief Engineer
D. Junior Typist
E. Chemist

15. The emphasis in public personnel administration during recent years has been less on the 15.___
A. need for the elimination of the spoils system and more on the development of policy and techniques of administration that contribute to employee selection and productivity
B. development of policy and techniques of administration that contribute to employee selection and productivity and more on the need for the elimination of the spoils system
C. human relation aspects of personnel administration and more on the technical problems of classification and placement
D. problems of personnel administration of governmental units in the United States and more on those of international organizations
E. problems of personnel administration in international organizations and more on those of governmental units in the United States

16. The recommendation has been made that explicit information be made available to all city employees concerning the procedure to be followed when appealing from a performance rating. 16.___
To put this recommendation into effect would be
A. *desirable*, primarily because employees would tend to have greater confidence in the performance rating system
B. *undesirable*, primarily because a greater number of employees would submit appeals with no merit
C. *desirable*, primarily because the additional publicity would spotlight the performance rating system
D. *undesirable*, primarily because all appeals should be treated as confidential matters and all efforts to make them public should be defeated
E. *desirable*, primarily because committing the appeal procedure to paper would tend to standardize it

17. The one of the following which in most cases is the BEST practical measure of the merits of the overall personnel policies of one organization as compared to the policies of similar organizations in the same area is the 17.___
   A. extent to which higher positions in the hierarchy are filled by career employees
   B. degree of loyalty and enthusiasm manifested by the work force
   C. rate at which replacements must be made in order to maintain the work force
   D. percentage of employees who have joined labor unions and the militancy of these unions
   E. scale of salaries

18. Classification may most properly be viewed as the building of a structure. 18.___
The fundamental unit in the classification structure is the
   A. assignment B. position C. service
   D. rank E. grade

19. The one of the following which is NOT usually included in a class specification is 19.___
   A. a definition of the duties and responsibilities covered
   B. the class title
   C. a description of the recruitment method to be used
   D. a statement of typical tasks performed
   E. the statement of minimum qualifications necessary to perform the work

20. The one of the following which is usually NOT considered part of a classification survey is 20.___
   A. grouping positions on the basis of similarities
   B. preparing job specifications
   C. analyzing and recording specific job duties
   D. adjusting job duties to employee qualifications
   E. allocating individual positions to classes

21. The one of the following which is MOST generally accepted as a prerequisite to the development of a sound career service is 21.___
   A. agreement to accept for all higher positions the senior eligible employee
   B. the recruitment of an adequate proportion of beginning employees who will eventually be capable of performing progressively more difficult duties
   C. strict adherence to the principle of competitive promotion from within for all positions above the entrance level
   D. the development of a program of periodically changing an employee's duties in order to prevent stagnation
   E. the existence of administrators who can stimulate employees and keep their production high

22. The determination of the fitness of a person to fill a position solely on the basis of his experience is 22.___
   A. *desirable*; experience is the best test of aptitude for a position when it is rated properly
   B. *undesirable*; the applicant may not be giving correct factual information in regard to his experience
   C. *desirable*; a uniform rating key can be applied to evaluate experience
   D. *undesirable*; it is difficult to evaluate from experience records how much the applicant has gained from his experience
   E. *desirable*; there will be more applicants for a position if no written or oral tests are required

23. The performance rating standards in a city department have been criticized by its employees as unfair. 23.___
The one of the following procedures which would probably be MOST effective in reducing this criticism is to
   A. publish a detailed statement showing how the standards were arrived at
   B. provide for participation by employee representatives in revising the standards
   C. allow individual employees to submit written statements about the standards employed
   D. arrange for periodic meetings of the entire staff at which the standards are discussed
   E. appoint a review board consisting of senior supervisory employees to reconsider the standards

24. The statement has been made that personnel administration is the MOST fundamental and important task of the head of any organization. 24.___
This statement is based, for the most part, on the fact that
   A. success or failure of an organization to reach its objectives depends on the attitudes and abilities of the people in the organization
   B. the influence of personnel administration on organization success varies in proportion to the number, the complexity, and the rarity of the virtues and qualities that are requisite to superior performance of the tasks involved
   C. a sound philosophy of personnel administration emphasizes the basic objective of superior service over any other consideration
   D. relative autonomy is permitted each department, particularly with respect to the handling of personnel
   E. diversity of personnel practices as to salaries, hours, etc., leads to poor morale

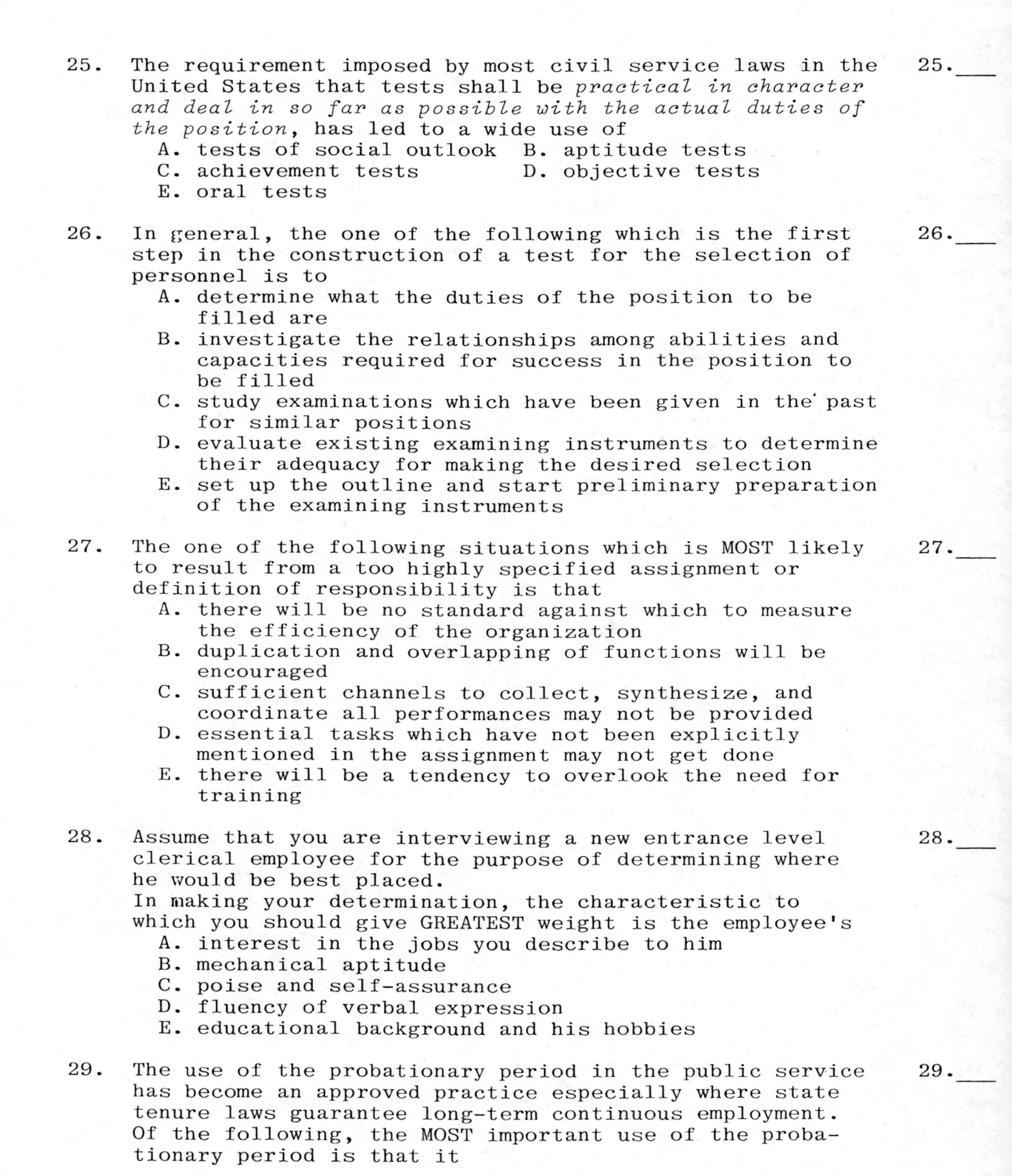

25. The requirement imposed by most civil service laws in the United States that tests shall be *practical in character and deal in so far as possible with the actual duties of the position*, has led to a wide use of 25.___
   A. tests of social outlook B. aptitude tests
   C. achievement tests D. objective tests
   E. oral tests

26. In general, the one of the following which is the first step in the construction of a test for the selection of personnel is to 26.___
   A. determine what the duties of the position to be filled are
   B. investigate the relationships among abilities and capacities required for success in the position to be filled
   C. study examinations which have been given in the past for similar positions
   D. evaluate existing examining instruments to determine their adequacy for making the desired selection
   E. set up the outline and start preliminary preparation of the examining instruments

27. The one of the following situations which is MOST likely to result from a too highly specified assignment or definition of responsibility is that 27.___
   A. there will be no standard against which to measure the efficiency of the organization
   B. duplication and overlapping of functions will be encouraged
   C. sufficient channels to collect, synthesize, and coordinate all performances may not be provided
   D. essential tasks which have not been explicitly mentioned in the assignment may not get done
   E. there will be a tendency to overlook the need for training

28. Assume that you are interviewing a new entrance level clerical employee for the purpose of determining where he would be best placed. 28.___
In making your determination, the characteristic to which you should give GREATEST weight is the employee's
   A. interest in the jobs you describe to him
   B. mechanical aptitude
   C. poise and self-assurance
   D. fluency of verbal expression
   E. educational background and his hobbies

29. The use of the probationary period in the public service has become an approved practice especially where state tenure laws guarantee long-term continuous employment. 29.___
Of the following, the MOST important use of the probationary period is that it

A. provides supervisory contact which will help the new employee regardless of retention at the end of the probationary period
B. supplies confirming evidence of academic and cultural fitness not measurable in formal test procedures
C. introduces the new employee to the office and the work situation which conditions future performance
D. provides the new employee with a sound basis for self-improvement
E. reveals aspects of performance and attitude toward the job not adequately measured by formal examination

30. The first prerequisite to the formulation of any compensation plan for a public agency is the collection and analysis of certain basic data. 30.___
Data are NOT usually collected for this purpose in regard to
A. working conditions in the agency
B. the wage paid in the agency at present
C. labor turnover in the agency
D. the cost of living in the area
E. the age and sex distribution of the employees

31. The one of the following personnel administration techniques which when properly utilized will yield information concerning current training needs of an organization is the 31.___
A. classification plan
B. performance rating
C. personnel register
D. compensation plan
E. employee handbook

32. In administering the activities of a personnel office with a staff of fifteen employees, including seven personnel technicians, the personnel officer should 32.___
A. delegate full authority and responsibility to each staff member and discharge those who do not meet his standards
B. endeavor to keep tab on the work of each individual on his staff
C. make sure each job is being done properly or do it himself
D. plan work programs, make assignments, and check on performance
E. concern himself only with major policies and expect subordinates to carry out actual functions

33. The one of the following factors which is MOST influential in determining the proportion of qualified applicants who refuse public employment when offered is the 33.___
A. interim between application and offer of a position
B. specific nature of the duties of the position
C. general nature of economic conditions at the time when the position is offered
D. salary paid
E. general undesirable nature of public employment

34. A placement officer in a department follows the procedure of consulting the supervisor of the unit in which a vacancy exists concerning the kind of worker he wants before attempting to fill the vacancy.
This procedure is, in general,
A. *undesirable*; it makes the selection process dependent on the whim of the supervisor
B. *desirable*; it will make for a more effectively working organization
C. *undesirable*; if the kind of worker the supervisor wants is not available, he will be dissatisfied
D. *desirable*; the more people who are consulted about a matter of this kind, the more chance there is that no mistake will be made
E. *undesirable*; the wishes of the worker as well as those of the supervisor should be taken into consideration

34.___

35. In a large organization, proper recruitment is not possible without the existence of an effective position classification system.
The one of the following which BEST explains why this is the case is that otherwise effective means of determining the capabilities and characteristics of prospective employees are of little value
A. unless these are related to the salary scale and current economic conditions
B. without a knowledge of the essential character of the work to be performed in each position
C. where no attempt to classify the different recruitment approaches has been made in advance
D. if there has been no attempt made to obtain the cooperation of the employees involved
E. to personnel officers who tend to place new employees in positions without reference to capabilities

35.___

36. The recommendation has been made that a departmental grievance board be set up, which would handle all employee grievances from their inception to conclusion.
Of the following comments for and against the acceptance of this recommendation, the one which is NOT valid is that it is
A. *desirable*, primarily because it will remove a constant source of friction between supervisor and employee and place the problem in the hands of an objective board
B. *undesirable*, primarily because handling grievances is an integral part of the supervisory process and the immediate supervisor must be afforded the opportunity to deal with the situation
C. *desirable*, primarily because no supervisor will have to determine whether he has been unfair to one of his subordinates and no subordinate will have a grievance
D. *desirable*, primarily because the handling of grievances will tend to be expedited as the board will have only one function
E. *undesirable*, primarily because the handling of grievances will tend to be delayed as the board will not have all the necessary information available

36.___

37. The one of the following which is frequently given as a major argument against a tightly knit promotion-from-within policy is that 37.___
   A. it takes too long for an employee in the lower grades to reach the top
   B. all persons both in and out of the government are equally entitled to civil service jobs
   C. persons are placed in executive jobs who are too well acquainted with the existing organization
   D. it leads to the presence in executive jobs of clerks who still operate as clerks
   E. it is not desirable to guarantee to all employees promotion to new responsibilities from time to time

38. Of the following factors which are influential in determining which employment a young man or woman will choose, government employ is generally considered superior in 38.___
   A. incentives to improve efficiency
   B. opportunities to move into other similar organizations
   C. prestige and recognition
   D. leave and retirement benefits
   E. salaries

39. Training programs, to be fully effective, should be concerned not only with the acquisition or improvement of skills but also with 39.___
   A. employee attitude and will to work
   B. the personality problems of the individual employees
   C. time and motion studies for the development of new procedures
   D. the recruitment of the best persons available to fill a given position
   E. such theoretical background material as is deemed necessary

Questions 40-45.

DIRECTIONS: Questions 40 through 45 are to be answered on the basis of the following paragraphs.

Plan 1 Hire broadly qualified people, work out their assignments from time to time to suit the needs of the enterprise and aptitudes of individuals. Let their progress and recognition be based on the length and overall quality of the service, regardless of the significance of individual assignments which they periodically assume.

Plan 2 Hire experts and assign them well-defined duties. Their compensation, for the most part, should be dependent on the duties performed.

40. For Plan 1 to be successful, there must be assured, to a much greater extent than for Plan 2, the existence of
   A. a well-developed training program
   B. a widely publicized recruitment program
   C. in general, better working conditions
   D. more skilled administrators
   E. a greater willingness to work together toward a common goal

40.___

41. Plan 1 would tend to develop employees who were
   A. dissatisfied because of the impossibility of advancing rapidly to positions of importance
   B. conversant only with problems in the particular field in which they were employed
   C. in general, not satisfied with the work they perform
   D. intensely competitive
   E. able to perform a variety of functions

41.___

42. Large governmental organizations in the United States tend, in general, to use Plan
   A. 1
   B. 2
   C. 1 for technical positions and Plan 2 for clerical positions
   D. 2 for administrative positions and Plan 1 for clerical and technical positions
   E. 1 for office machine operators and Plan 2 for technical positions

42.___

43. In organizations which operate on the basis of Plan 1, placement of a man in the proper job after selection is much more difficult than in those which operate on the basis of Plan 2.
This statement is, in general,
   A. *correct*; the organization would have only specific positions open and generalists would be forced into technical positions
   B. *not correct*; specific aptitudes and abilities would tend to be determined in advance as would be the case with Plan 2
   C. *correct*; it is much more difficult to determine specific aptitudes and abilities than general qualifications
   D. *not correct*; placement would be based on the needs of the organization, consequently only a limited number of positions would be available
   E. *correct*; the selection is not on the basis of specific aptitudes and abilities

43.___

44. Administration in an organization operating on the basis of Plan 1 would tend to be less flexible than one operating on the basis of Plan 2.
This statement is, in general,

44.___

A. *correct*; recruitment of experts permits rapid expansion
B. *not correct*; the absence of well-defined positions permits wide and rapid recruitment without an extensive selection period
C. *correct*; well-defined positions allow for replacement on an assembly-line basis without an extensive breaking-in period and thus permits greater flexibility
D. *not correct*; Plan 1 presents greater freedom in movement of individuals from one position to another and in re-defining positions according to capabilities of employees and the needs of the moment
E. *correct*; Plan 1 presents greater freedom in adjusting an organizational structure to unexpected stresses since the clear definition of duties shows where the danger points are

45. To a greater extent than Plan 2, Plan 1 leads to conflict and overlapping in administrative operations. 45.___
In general, this is the case because
A. employees paid on the basis of duties performed tend to be more conscious of overlapping operations and tend to limit their activities
B. experts refuse to accept responsibilities in fields other than their own
C. the lack of carefully defined positions may conceal many points at which coordination and reconciliation are necessary
D. there tends to be more pressure for *empire building* where prestige is measured solely in terms of assignment
E. there is less need, under Plan 1, to define lines of responsibility and authority and consequently conflict will arise

46. Some organizations interview employees who resign or are discharged. 46.___
This procedure is USUALLY
A. of great value in reducing labor turnover and creating good will toward the organization
B. of little or no value as the views of incompetent or disgruntled employees are of questionable validity
C. dangerous; it gives employees who are leaving an organization the opportunity to pay off old scores
D. of great value in showing the way to more efficient methods of production and the establishment of higher work norms
E. dangerous; it may lead to internal friction as operating departments believe that it is not the function of the personnel office to check on operations

47. The one of the following which is the MOST common flaw in the administration of an employee performance rating system is the 47.___
   A. failure to explain the objectives of the system to employees
   B. lack of safeguards to prevent supervisors from rating employees down for personal reasons
   C. tendency for rating supervisors to rate their employees much too leniently
   D. fact that employees are aware of the existence of the system
   E. increasing number of committees and boards required

48. As a result of its study of the operations of the Federal government, the Hoover Commission recommended that, for purposes of reduction in force, employees be ranked from the standpoint of their overall usefulness to the agency in question. 48.___
The one of the following which is a major disadvantage of this proposal is that it would probably result in
   A. efficient employees becoming indifferent to the social problems posed
   B. a sense of insecurity on the part of employees which might tend to lower efficiency
   C. the retention of employees who are at or just past their peak performance
   D. the retention of generalists rather than specialists
   E. the loss of experience in the agency, as ability rather than knowledge will be the criterion

49. A personnel officer checking the turnover rate in his department found that, over a period of five years, the rate at which engineers left the organization was exactly the same as the rate at which junior clerks left the department. 49.___
This information tends to indicate
   A. that something may be amiss with the organization; the rate for engineers under ordinary circumstances should be higher than for clerks
   B. that the organization is in good shape; neither the technical nor clerical aspects are being over-emphasized
   C. nothing which would be of value in determining the state of the organization
   D. that the organization is in good shape; working conditions, in general, are equivalent for all employees
   E. that something may be amiss with the organization; the turnover rate for engineers under ordinary circumstances should be lower than for clerks

50. Of the following, the MOST essential feature of a grievance procedure is that 50.___
A. those who appeal be assured of expert counsel
B. the administration have opportunity to review cases early in the procedure
C. it afford assurance that those who use it will not be discriminated against
D. general grievances be publicized
E. it be simple to administer

KEY (CORRECT ANSWERS)

1. B	11. E	21. B	31. B	41. E
2. E	12. C	22. D	32. D	42. B
3. A	13. A	23. B	33. A	43. E
4. D	14. D	24. A	34. B	44. D
5. A	15. A	25. C	35. B	45. C
6. D	16. A	26. A	36. B	46. A
7. E	17. C	27. D	37. D	47. C
8. D	18. B	28. A	38. D	48. B
9. D	19. C	29. E	39. A	49. E
10. D	20. D	30. E	40. A	50. C

TEST 2

DIRECTIONS: Each question or incomplete statement is followed by several suggested answers or completions. Select the one that BEST answers the question or completes the statement. *PRINT THE LETTER OF THE CORRECT ANSWER IN THE SPACE AT THE RIGHT.*

1. In which of the following fields could two or more groups duplicating each other's work USUALLY be best justified? 1.____
   A. Accounting
   B. Personnel
   C. Public relations
   D. Research and development
   E. Systems and procedures

2. Which of the following statements is MOST nearly accurate? A(The) span of control 2.____
   A. of 5 people is better than that of 10 people
   B. of 5 people may be better or worse than that of 10 people
   C. of 5 people is worse than that of 10 people
   D. is rarely over 20 minutes at any one time
   E. means the same as the scalar system

3. A linear responsibility chart is 3.____
   A. a graphical method of showing each sub-project making up a total project with the time it takes to complete each
   B. a graphical method of showing jobs, functions, and, by the use of appropriate symbols, the relationship of each job to each function
   C. a graphical method of solving linear equations used in doing Operations Research
   D. a new method of procedures analysis which makes it possible to focus on both the employees and the equipment they use
   E. another name for a special organization chart

4. An administrator of a public agency is faced with the problem of deciding which of two divisions should be responsible for the statistical reporting of the agency. This work is now located in one of them but each of the two division chiefs believes that the work should be located within his division because of its relationship to other activities under his supervision. The Organization Planning Section is located in one of the two divisions.
   Assuming that in this situation the administrator can select any one of the following courses of action, the BEST for him to take would be to 4.____
   A. assign a staff member from the Organization Planning Section to study the problem, who for the duration of the assignment would report directly to the administrator

B. assign staff from the Organization Planning Section to study the problem
C. assign the statistical work to the other division for a trial period because of the problems which exist under the present arrangement
D. call in an outside consultant or refer it to a competent staff employee not assigned to the divisions involved
E. leave the organization as it is because the advantages of a change are not entirely clear to all concerned

5. The problem of whether office services such as filing, duplicating, and stenography should be centralized or decentralized arises in every business organization. One advantage of decentralizing these services is that 5.____
A. greater facility exists in such matters as finding correspondence
B. greater flexibility exists in rotating workers during vacations
C. higher production is attained at a lower cost per unit
D. knowledge of the purpose and use of work acts as an incentive for production
E. reduction in investment results from the use of less machinery

6. Research to date on the relationship between productivity and morale shows that 6.____
A. high productivity and high morale nearly always go together
B. high productivity and low morale nearly always go together
C. low productivity and high morale nearly always go together
D. low productivity and low morale nearly always go together
E. there is no clear relationship between productivity and morale

7. Which one of the following statements BEST describes *work measurement* as commonly used in government? 7.____
It is
A. a method of establishing an equitable relationship between volume of work performed and manpower utilized
B. a new technique which may be substituted for traditional accounting methods
C. the amount of work turned out by an organization in a given time period
D. the same as the work count, as used in Work Simplification
E. the same as time-motion study

8. Critics of work measurement have contended that any increase in production is more than offset by deterioration in standards of quality or service. 8.____
The BEST answer to this charge is to
   A. argue that increases in production have not been offset by decreased quality
   B. define work units in terms of both quality and quantity
   C. ignore it
   D. point out that statistical quality control can be used to control quality
   E. point out that work measurement is not concerned with quality, and hence that the argument is irrelevant

9. When it is determined that a given activity or process is so intangible that it cannot be reflected adequately by a work unit, it is BEST for a work measurement system to 9.____
   A. combine that activity with others that are measurable
   B. discuss the activity only in narrative reports
   C. exclude it from the work measurement system
   D. include only the time devoted to that activity or process
   E. select the best available work unit, as better than none

10. Which one of the following is frequently referred to as the father of Statistical Quality Control? 10.____
   A. Ralph M. Barnes
   B. John M. Pfiffner
   C. Benjamin Selekman
   D. Walter A. Shewhart
   E. Donald C. Stone

11. Which one of the following BEST explains the use and value of the *upper control limit* (and *lower control limit* where applicable) in Statistical Quality Control? 11.____
It
   A. automatically keeps production under control
   B. indicates that unit costs are too high or too low
   C. is useful as a training device for new workers
   D. tells what pieces to discard or errors to correct
   E. tells when assignable causes as distinguished from chance causes are at work

12. A manager skilled in human relations can BEST be defined as one who 12.____
   A. can identify interpersonal problems and work out solutions to them
   B. can persuade people to do things his way
   C. gets along well with people and has many friends
   D. plays one role with his boss, another with his subordinates, and a third with his peers
   E. treats everyone fairly

13. The BEST way to secure efficient management is to 13.___
    A. allow staff agencies to solve administrative problems
    B. equip line management to solve its own problems
    C. get employees properly classified and trained
    D. prescribe standard operating procedures
    E. set up a board of control

14. The composition of the work force in American government and industry is changing. There has been an increase in the proportion of white collar to blue collar employees and an increase in the proportion of higher educated to lower educated employees. 14.___
    This change will MOST likely result in
    A. a more simplified forms control system
    B. closer supervision of employees
    C. further decentralization of decision-making
    D. more employee grievances
    E. organization by process instead of purpose

15. In which of the following professional journals would you be MOST apt to find articles on organization theory? 15.___
    A. Administrative Science Quarterly
    B. Factory Management and Maintenance
    C. Harvard Business Review
    D. O and M
    E. Public Administration Review

16. Which of the following organizations is MOST noted for its training courses in various management subjects? 16.___
    A. American Management Association
    B. American Political Science Association
    C. American Society for Public Administration
    D. Society for the Advancement of Management
    E. Systems and Procedures Association

17. A *performance budget* puts emphasis on 17.___
    A. achieving greatest economy
    B. expenditures for salaries, travel, rent, supplies, etc.
    C. revenues rather than on expenditures
    D. tables of organization or staffing patterns
    E. what is accomplished, e.g., number of applications processed, trees planted, buildings inspected, etc.

18. Which of the following statements MOST accurately defines *Operations Research*? 18.___
    A. A highly sophisticated reporting system used in the analysis of management problems
    B. A specialized application of electronic data processing in the analysis of management problems
    C. Research on operating problems
    D. Research on technological problems
    E. The application of sophisticated mathematical tools to the analysis of management problems

19. Which of the following characteristics of a system would MOST likely lead to the conclusion that manual methods should be used rather than punch card equipment? 19.___
    A. High volume
    B. Low volume but complex computations
    C. Operations of a fixed sequence
    D. Relatively simple work
    E. Repetitive work

20. Assume that an electronic wordprocessing typewriter costs $1100 and an electric typewriter costs $300. Except for speed of production, assume that in all other pertinent respects they are the same, including a life expectancy of 10 years each. 20.___
    What is the approximate amount of time $7.40 per hour typist must save and re-invest in work to have her word processor recoup the difference in purchase price?
    A. 11 hours annually
    B. 110 hours annually
    C. 550 hours annually
    D. 1100 hours annually
    E. One hour a day

21. The principal justification for using office machines to replace hand labor is to 21.___
    A. achieve automation
    B. eliminate errors
    C. increase productivity
    D. make work easier
    E. reduce labor problems

22. An analog computer is one which 22.___
    A. is classified as *medium* size
    B. is used primarily for solving scientific and engineering problems rather than for data processing
    C. operates on the principle of creating a physical, often electrical, analogy of the mathematical problem to be solved
    D. uses transistors rather than vacuum tubes
    E. works on the basis of logarithms

23. The binary numbering system used in computers is one which 23.___
    A. is much more complicated than the usual decimal numbering system
    B. uses a radix or base of 8
    C. uses letters of the alphabet rather than numerical digits
    D. uses only two digits, 0 and 1
    E. uses the customary ten digits, 0 through 9

24. An electronic computer performs various arithmetic operations by 24.___
    A. adding and subtracting
    B. adding, subtracting, dividing, and multiplying
    C. Boolean algebra
    D. multiplying and dividing
    E. all operations listed in B and C

25. The MOST effective basis for an analysis of the flow of work in a large governmental agency is the 25.___
A. analysis of descriptions written by employees
B. discussion of routines with selected employees
C. discussion of operations with supervisors
D. initiation of a series of general staff meetings to discuss operational procedures
E. observation of actual operations

26. The BEST reason for prescribing definite procedures for certain work in an organization is to 26.___
A. enable supervisor to keep *on top of* details of work
B. enable work to be processed speedily and consistently
C. facilitate incorporation of new policies
D. prevent individual discretion
E. reduce training periods

27. Which one of the following is the MOST important difference between clerks in small offices and those in large offices? 27.___
Clerks in
A. large offices are less closely supervised
B. large offices have more freedom to exercise originality in their work
C. small offices are more restricted by standardized procedures
D. small offices are more specialized in their duties
E. small offices need a greater variety of clerical skills

28. After taking the necessary steps to analyze a situation, an employee reaches a decision which is reviewed by his supervisor and found to be incorrect. 28.___
Of the following possible methods of dealing with this incident, the MOST constructive for the employee would be for the supervisor to
A. correct the decision and give the employee an explanation
B. correct the decision and suggest more detailed analysis in the future
C. help the employee discover what is wrong with the basis for decision
D. set up a temporary control on this type of decision until the employee demonstrates he can handle it
E. suggest that the employee review future cases of this type with him before reaching a decision

29. Which one of the following is NOT a purpose ordinarily served by charts? 29.___
A. Aid in training employees
B. Assist in presenting and selling recommendations
C. Detect gaps or discrepancies in data collected
D. Put facts in proper relationships to each other
E. Show up problems of human relationships

30. Which of the following descriptive statements does NOT constitute a desirable standard in evaluating an administrative sequence or series of tasks having a definite objective? 30.___
   A. All material should be routed as directly as possible to reduce the cost of time and motion.
   B. Each form must clear the section chief before going to another section.
   C. Each task should be assigned to the lowest-ranking employee who can perform it adequately.
   D. Each task should contribute positively to the basic purpose of the sequence.
   E. Similar tasks should be combined.

31. Which one of the following is NOT a principle of motion economy? 31.___
   A. Continuous curved motions are preferable to straight-line motions involving sudden and sharp changes in direction.
   B. Motions of the arms should be made in the same direction and should be made simultaneously.
   C. The hands should be relieved of all work that can be performed more advantageously by the feet.
   D. The two hands should begin and complete their motions at the same time.
   E. Two or more tools should be combined whenever possible.

32. Generally, the first step in the measurement of relative efficiency of office employees engaged in machine operation is the 32.___
   A. analysis of the class of positions involved to determine the duties and responsibilities and minimum qualifications necessary for successful job performance
   B. analysis of those skills which make for difference in the production of various employees
   C. development of a service rating scale which can be scored accurately
   D. development of a standard unit of production that can be widely applied and that will give comparable data
   E. selection of an appropriate sampling of employees whose duties involve the specific factors to be measured

33. In the course of a survey, a disgruntled employee of Unit A comes to your office with an offer to *tell all* about Unit B, where he used to work.
You should 33.___
   A. listen to him but ignore any statements he makes
   B. listen to him carefully, but verify his assertions before acting on them
   C. make him speak to you in the presence of the persons he is criticizing
   D. reprimand him for not minding his own business
   E. report him to the security officer

34. Combining several different procedures into a single flow of work would MOST likely achieve which of the following advantages? 34.___
   A. Better teamwork
   B. Higher quality decisions
   C. Improved morale
   D. Reduced fluctuations in workload
   E. Reduced problems of control

35. After conducting a systems survey in the Personnel Division you find that there is not sufficient work in the Division to keep a recently hired employee gainfully employed. 35.___
The BEST solution to this problem is usually to
   A. lay off the employee with a full month's salary
   B. leave the employee in the Division because the workload may increase
   C. leave the employee in the Personnel Division, but assign him overflow work from other divisions
   D. reassign the employee when an appropriate opening occurs elsewhere in the organization
   E. request the employee to resign so that no unfavorable references will appear on his personnel record

36. You are making a study of a central headquarters office which processes claims received from a number of regional offices. You notice the following problems: some employees are usually busy while others assigned to the same kind of work in the same grade have little to do; high-level professional people frequently spend considerable time searching for files in the file room. 36.___
Which of the following charts would be MOST useful to record and analyze the data needed to help solve these problems?
_____ chart.
   A. Forms distribution
   B. Layout
   C. Operation
   D. Process
   E. Work distribution

37. A *therblig* is BEST defined as a
   A. follower of Frederick W. Taylor
   B. small element or task of an operation used in time-motion study
   C. special type of accounting machine used to sort punch cards
   D. type of curve used in charting certain mathematical relationships
   E. unit for measuring the effectiveness of air-conditioning

38. One of the following advantages which is LEAST likely to accrue to a large organization as a result of establishing a centralized typing and stenographic unit is that 38.____
   A. less time is wasted
   B. morale of the stenographers increases
   C. the stenographers receive better training
   D. wages are more consistent
   E. work is more equally distributed

39. In the communications process, the work *noise* is used to refer to 39.____
   A. anything that interferes with the message between transmitter and receiver
   B. meaningless communications
   C. the amplitude of verbal communication
   D. the level of general office and environmental sounds other than specific verbal communications
   E. the product of the grapevine

40. Which of the following is NOT an advantage of oral instructions as compared with written instructions when dealing with a small group? 40.____
   A. Oral instructions are more adaptable to complex orders.
   B. Oral instructions can be changed more easily and quickly.
   C. Oral instructions facilitate exchange of information between the order giver and order receiver.
   D. Oral instructions make it easier for order giver and order receiver.
   E. The oral medium is suitable for instructions that will be temporary.

41. The employee opinion or attitude survey has for some time been accepted as a valuable communications device.
Of the following, the benefit which is LEAST likely to occur from the use of such a survey is: 41.____
   A. A clearer view of employee understanding of management policies is obtained
   B. Improved morale may result
   C. Information useful for supervisory and executive development is obtained
   D. The reasons why management policies were adopted are clarified
   E. Useful comparisons can be made between organization units

42. Which of the following is the MOST important principle to remember in preparing written reports that are to be submitted to a superior? 42.____
   A. Avoid mentioning in writing errors or mistakes
   B. Include human interest anecdotes
   C. Put all information into graphical or tabular form
   D. Report everything that has happened
   E. Report results in relation to plan

43. In conducting an electronic data processing study, with which one of the following should you be LEAST concerned? 43.___
   A. Computer characteristics; i.e., word length requirements, type storage characteristics, etc.
   B. Data collection requirements
   C. Methods used by other governmental jurisdictions
   D. System input/output requirements and volume
   E. System integration and flow of work

44. The MOST significant difference between a random access and a sequential type data processing computer system is: 44.___
   A. Generally, a random access system has lower *locating* or access times
   B. Random access provides the potential for processing data on a *first come-first served* basis without the necessity of batching or pre-arranging the data in some sequence
   C. Random access systems are more often disk type storage systems
   D. Random access systems can operate more easily in conjunction with sequential tape or card oriented computer systems
   E. Random access systems have larger storage capacities

45. The most effective leader would MOST likely be one who 45.___
   A. is able to use a variety of leadership styles depending on the circumstances
   B. issues clear, forceful directives
   C. knows the substance of the work better than any of his subordinates
   D. supervises his subordinates closely
   E. uses democratic methods

46. One large office is a more efficient operating unit than the same number of square feet split into smaller offices. Of the following, the one that does NOT support this statement is: 46.___
   A. Better light and ventilation are possible
   B. Changes in layout are less apt to be made thus avoiding disruption of work flow
   C. Communication between individual employees is more direct
   D. Space is more fully utilized
   E. Supervision and control are more easily maintained

47. The major purpose for adopting specific space standards is to 47.___
   A. allocate equal space to employees doing the same kind of work
   B. cut costs
   C. keep space from becoming a status symbol
   D. prevent empire-building
   E. provide an accurate basis for charging for space allocated to each organization unit

48. The modular concept in office space planning is 48.___
  A. a method of pre-planning office space for economical use
  B. expensive because it complicates the air conditioning and electrical systems
  C. outdated because it lacks flexibility
  D. used as a basis for planning future space requirements
  E. used primarily for executive offices

49. Which one of the following statements is NOT correct? 49.___
  A. A general conference or committee room may eliminate the need for a number of private offices.
  B. In designing office space the general trend is toward the use of a standard color scheme.
  C. Private offices should be constructed in such a way as to avoid cutting off natural light and ventilation.
  D. Private offices result in a larger investment in equipment and furnishings.
  E. Transparent or translucent glass can be used in the upper portion of the partition for private offices.

50. Which one of the following is NOT a good general rule of communications in an organization? 50.___
  A. All supervisors should know the importance of communications.
  B. Oral communications are better than written where persuasion is needed.
  C. People should be told facts that make them feel they *belong*.
  D. The grapevine should be eliminated.
  E. The supervisor should hear information before his subordinates.

KEY (CORRECT ANSWERS)

1. D	11. E	21. C	31. B	41. D
2. B	12. A	22. C	32. D	42. E
3. B	13. B	23. D	33. B	43. C
4. D	14. C	24. A	34. D	44. B
5. D	15. A	25. E	35. D	45. A
6. E	16. A	26. B	36. E	46. B
7. A	17. E	27. E	37. B	47. A
8. B	18. E	28. C	38. B	48. A
9. D	19. B	29. E	39. A	49. B
10. D	20. A	30. B	40. A	50. D

EXAMINATION SECTION

TEST 1

DIRECTIONS: Each question or incomplete statement is followed by several suggested answers or completions. Select the one that BEST answers the question or completes the statement. *PRINT THE LETTER OF THE CORRECT ANSWER IN THE SPACE AT THE RIGHT.*

1. The Public Services Careers Program is a manpower program 1.___
   A. designed to develop permanent employment opportunities for the disadvantaged
   B. designed to encourage college graduates to enter the field of public administration
   C. run by the federal government for private organizations
   D. designed to prepare physically handicapped persons for new positions

2. The Intergovernmental Personnel Act (P.L. 91-648) provides federal assistance to state and local governments for improving and strengthening personnel administration. 2.___
   The one of the following which is NOT provided for in this Act is
   A. creation of a new personnel system for upper-level personnel
   B. expanded training programs
   C. improved personnel management
   D. interchange of employees between federal government and state and local governments

3. Kepner-Tregoc management training courses are MOST closely involved with 3.___
   A. management by objectives
   B. development of overall leadership qualities
   C. leadership style
   D. problem-solving techniques

4. The BASIC purpose of the Managerial Grid for training program is to train managers to 4.___
   A. have concern for both production and the people who produce
   B. utilize scientific problem-solving techniques
   C. maximize efficient communication
   D. improve the quality of their leadership in *brainstorming* sessions

5. In establishing employee development objectives, management must make sure that they are 5.___
   A. stated in broad terms
   B. relevant to job performance
   C. developed by a training expert
   D. written in the vocabulary of the training field

6. In order that group conferences serve their purpose of developing professional staff, it is essential that 6.___
   A. discussion of controversial matters be limited
   B. notes be taken by the participants
   C. participants be encouraged to take part in the discussions
   D. chairmanships be rotated at the meetings

7. A personnel officer receives a request to conduct a course for interested employees who have filed for a promotion examination. The request that the course be given on agency time is turned down. 7.___
   This action is
   A. *justified*; such courses do not contain content that serve to improve employee performance
   B. *justified*; the course is designed to benefit the individual primarily, not the agency
   C. *unjustified*; regardless of objective, any training related to City operations will have an affect on employee performance tangibly or intangibly
   D. *unjustified*; if productivity has been based on full use of employee time, productivity will suffer if time is allocated for such a course

8. Of the following, the PRIMARY objective of sensitivity training is to 8.___
   A. teach management principles to participants
   B. improve and refine the decision-making process
   C. give the participants insight as to how they are perceived by others
   D. improve the emotional stability of the participants

9. In considering the functions of a manager, it is clear that the FIRST step in building a quality work force is the manager's need to 9.___
   A. design jobs to meet the realities of the labor market
   B. examine the qualification requirements for his positions and eliminate those which appear to be controversial
   C. determine the methods to be used in reaching that special public deemed most suitable for the agency
   D. establish controls so that there is reasonable assurance that the plans established to staff the agency will be properly consummated

10. Based on data documenting the differences between healthy and unhealthy organizations, which statement describes a HEALTHY, as contrasted with an unhealthy, organization? 10.___
   A. Innovation is not widespread but exists in the hands of a few.
   B. Risks are not avoided but accepted as a condition of change.
   C. Decision-making is not dispersed but delegated to organizational levels.
   D. Conflict is not overt but resolved without confrontation.

11. Which of the following management actions is NOT conducive to greater job satisfaction? 11.___
    A. Diversifying tasks in the unit as much as feasible
    B. Permitting workers to follow through on tasks rather than carry out single segments of the process
    C. Avoiding the use of *project teams* or *task forces*
    D. Delegating authority to each layer of the hierarchy to the maximum extent possible

12. When the span of control of a manager or administrator is widened or increased, a MOST likely result is 12.___
    A. greater specificity of operational procedures
    B. a decrease in total worker-administrator contacts
    C. a blurring of objectives and goals
    D. an increase in responsibility of subordinates

13. Although *superagencies* may have value in assisting the chief executive to supervise operations more efficiently, a MAJOR shortcoming is that they 13.___
    A. may not provide more effective delivery of services to the public
    B. may limit the chief executive in his ability to find out what is happening within the agencies
    C. tend to reduce the responsibility of component agency heads for their own operations
    D. add costs that have little relation to the efforts to achieve administrative effectiveness

14. Business and psychological literature on managerial effectiveness is based for the MOST part on 14.___
    A. job analyses or descriptions about the management process
    B. field studies or observations about the outcome of effective management
    C. personal experiences or opinions about the traits good managers possess
    D. attitudes or perceptions of managers about organizational goals and strategies

15. The impression MOST likely to be gained from published surveys of traits necessary for management is that the lists 15.___
    A. limit identified traits to obvious human virtues
    B. lack precision in pinpointing behavioral elements
    C. emphasize negative rather than positive variables
    D. exclude attitudinal and motivational factors

16. Management concepts in public and private organizations have been undergoing drastic shifts as a consequence of a new view emerging from the recent synthesis of learning in the sciences. While still in its infancy, this development has challenged much of what has been considered accepted management theory for a long time. 16.___
    This change is frequently referred to in current management literature as
    A. systems thinking
    B. scientific management
    C. behavioral science
    D. multivariate analysis

17. Assuming more and more importance every day, the subject of management has undergone prodigious change in recent times. 17.___
With respect to this development, the MOST valid expression concerning the current status of management would be:
   A. Authoritative texts have progressed to the point where differences in the formal treatment of the process of management are comparatively rare
   B. The generalized theory of management which has been synthesized recently by scholars in the field has given the term *management* a fixed meaning and definition from which revolutionary progress may now be anticipated
   C. Unity of conception, thought, and view about the process of management is still a long way off
   D. Unity of conception, thought, and view about the process of management has been achieved in administrative circles under the revolutionary concepts brought into being as a result of the latest developments in computer technology

18. That there is no average man, the manager would be first to acknowledge. Yet the exigencies of organized enterprise require that the assumption be made. 18.___
Of the following, the procedure or process that is PRIMARILY based on this assumption is the
   A. administration of discipline
   B. establishment of rules and regulations
   C. policy of job enlargement
   D. promotion policy

19. There are four or more phases in the process of manpower planning. 19.___
Of the following, the one which should be scheduled FIRST is
   A. gathering and analyzing data through manpower inventories and forecasts
   B. establishing objectives and policies through personnel and budget control units
   C. designing plan and action programs
   D. establishing production goals for the agency

20. When ranked in order of frequency of performance, studies show which of the following ranks LOWEST among the functions performed by central personnel offices in local governments? 20.___
   A. Planning, conducting, and coordinating training
   B. Certifying or auditing payrolls
   C. Conducting personnel investigations
   D. Engaging in collective bargaining

21. Which of the following activities of an agency personnel division can BEST be considered a control function? 21.___
   A. Scheduling safety meetings for supervisory staff
   B. Consultation on a disciplinary problem
   C. Reminders to line units to submit personnel evaluations
   D. Processing requests for merit increases

22. Which of the following interview styles is MOST appropriate for use in a problem-solving situation? 22.____
   A. Directed
   B. Non-directive
   C. Stress
   D. Authoritarian

23. Which of the following is a COMMONLY used measure of morale in an organization? 23.____
   A. Turnover rate
   B. Espirit de corps
   C. Specialized division of labor
   D. Job satisfaction

24. According to studies in personnel and industrial psychology, information that travels along the *grapevine* or informal communication system in an organization usually follows a pattern BEST classified as 24.____
   A. cluster - key informants tell several individuals, one of whom passes it on in the same way
   B. wheel - around through successive informants until it reaches the source
   C. chain - double informants linked to successive pairs
   D. random probability - informant tells anyone he happens to encounter, and so forth

25. A carefully devised program has been developed in a certain city for combining performance evaluation and seniority into a formula to determine order of layoff. The essence of this plan is first to group employees of a particular job class into *seniority blocks* and then to use performance evaluation as a basis for determining layoff order within each seniority block. 25.____
The BEST of the following inferences which can be made from the above paragraph is that
   A. this plan is unfair since seniority is not given sufficient weight in the selection process
   B. this city is probably behind most civil service jurisdictions in the evaluation of employee performance
   C. combining performance and seniority cannot be done since it is like *combining apples and oranges*
   D. under this plan, it is conceivable that a person with high seniority could be laid off before a person with lower seniority

26. With any decentralization of personnel functions, specific procedures and rules are developed to assure conformance with relevant provisions of the Civil Service Law and the Rules and Regulations of the central personnel agency. 26.____
To the extent that these procedures are specific and detailed,
   A. agency involvement in the execution of the decentralized function will be limited
   B. agency discretion in the administration of the decentralized function will be limited
   C. size and composition of agency personnel staff will tend to become fixed
   D. flexibility of application to bolster agency performance will be provided

27. While decentralization of personnel functions to give operating agencies more authority in personnel matters relating to their operations has been a goal of personnel policy, recentralization is an ever-present possibility. Of the following, the factor which is the BEST indicator of the desirability of recentralization is that 27.___
    A. inconsistent policies or inconsistent application of policies resulted when decentralized operations were instituted
    B. costs in terms of personnel and procedures increased significantly when decentralization was introduced
    C. the decentralization did not serve any real identifiable need
    D. agency personnel units were not prepared to handle the responsibilities delegated to them

28. Although the Department of Personnel has developed and maintains an Executive Roster, its use by agency heads to fill managerial positions has been disappointing. Of the following, the one that is the LEAST likely reason for NOT using the roster is that 28.___
    A. personal factors essential to the relationship of manager and administrator are not revealed in the roster record
    B. most agencies prefer to advance their own employees rather than use a general roster
    C. some agency heads think of experienced City managerial employees as superannuated administrative deadwood
    D. use of the roster implies a reduction of the scope of administrative discretion in selection

29. During one program year, an examiner found a number of occasions in which a special task, a special report, or some activity outside of planned programs had to be assigned. One staff member continually offered to undertake these assignments whenever the administrative examiner requested a volunteer. He handled these jobs in timely fashion even though he had begun the year with a full-time workload. Of the following, the conclusion MOST warranted from the information given is that the 29.___
    A. staff member was much more efficient than other examiners in the division in planning and executing work
    B. staff member's regular workload actually was less than a full-time assignment for him
    C. commitment and will to serve was greater in this member than in others
    D. quality of work of other examiners may have been higher than that of this staff member

30. An examiner has three subordinate supervisors, each responsible for a major program in his division. He finds that one supervisor is much weaker than the other two, both in his planning of work and in his follow-through to achieve timely completion of tasks. To bolster the *weak* supervisor, the administrative examiner reassigns his best examiners to this unit. 30.___

This decision is POOR primarily because
- A. the performance of the competent examiners is likely to suffer eventually
- B. the assigned examiners will be expected to make more decisions themselves
- C. the ineffective supervisor might have done better by assignment elsewhere
- D. indicated disciplinary action was not taken

31. Because of the frustrations felt by many public administrators who have been unable to motivate their subordinates, the classic civil service reform movement has been condemned by observers of the public government scene. Those condemning that movement believe that the system has failed to develop a quality public service precisely because of the policies implemented as a result of the reform movement. 31.___
They suggest that the remedy lies in
    - A. centralizing the personnel functions in the hands of an elite group of professional personnel practitioners who would be best equipped to initiate needed remedies
    - B. changing the concept of personnel management to a generalist approach, thus guaranteeing a broader and more integrated resolution of employee problems
    - C. finding and implementing more practical personnel techniques in dealing with the various functional personnel areas
    - D. completely decentralizing personnel administration to the responsible agency heads

32. The British scholar and statesman Harold J. Laski has stated that the expert was too likely to *make his subject the measure of life, instead of making life the measure of his subject.* 32.___
When applying this comment to the modern public service administrator, it is meant that the administrator should
    - A. expand the jurisdiction of his authority so that better integration among functional areas is possible
    - B. personally be receptive to the concept of change and not merely concerned with protecting the methods of the past
    - C. develop a group of specialists in functional subject matter areas in order to give better service to the operating department heads
    - D. see the relationship of his own particular area of jurisdiction to other governmental activities and to the private sector

33. Suppose that, as an examiner, you are asked to prepare a budget for the next fiscal year for a division performing personnel functions. 33.___
Of the following, the consideration which is LEAST important to your development of the division budget involves
    - A. adequacy of the current year's budget for your division
    - B. changes in workload that can be anticipated

C. budget restrictions that have been indicated in a memorandum covering budget preparation
D. staff reassignments which are expected during that fiscal year

34. Suppose you have been designated chairman of an intra-departmental committee to implement a major policy decision. The one of the following which is LEAST desirable as a subject for a planning meeting is 34.___
A. determination of details of execution by each bureau
B. specific allocation of responsibility for the phases of administration
C. provision of means for coordination and follow-up
D. formulation of sub-goals for each bureau

35. Collective bargaining challenges the concept of the neutrality of the personnel function in the public service. Which one of the following statements BEST reflects this observation? 35.___
A. Personnel offices must clearly serve as a bridge between management and employees.
B. In most cases, negotiation involves a tripartite group - labor relations, fiscal or budget, and the employee organization.
C. Personnel bureaus must be identified openly with the public employer.
D. Personnel units cannot make policy or commitments in labor relations; their primary function is to execute personnel decisions made by others.

36. Changes in the field of public employee labor relations have been both numerous and significant in recent years. Below are four statements that an examiner preparing a report on developments in this area of personnel management might possibly include as correct: 36.___
I. At least one-third of the states give some type of bargaining rights to their employees
II. Less than half the states have granted public employees the right to organize
III. Since 1959, at least eight states have enacted comprehensive labor relations laws affecting public employees
IV. By 1966, state and local governments had entered into more than 1,000 separate agreements with employee organizations

Which of the following choices lists the statements that are CORRECT?
A. I, II, and III are correct, but not IV
B. I, III, and IV are correct, but not II
C. I and III are correct, but not II and IV
D. II and III are correct, but not I and IV

37. Which of the following is NOT a major goal of unions in contract negotiations? 37.___
A. Establishing management prerogatives
B. Preserving and strengthening the union

C. Promoting social and economic objectives
D. Promoting the status of the union representatives

Questions 38-39.

DIRECTIONS: Answer Questions 38 and 39 on the basis of the following paragraph.

An impending reorganization within an agency will mean loss by transfer of several professional staff members from the personnel division. The division chief is asked to designate the persons to be transferred. After reviewing the implications of this reduction of staff with his assistant, the division chief discussed the matter at a staff meeting. He adopts the recommendations of several staff members to have volunteers make up the required reduction.

38. The decision to permit personnel to volunteer for transfer is 38.___
A. *poor*; it is not likely that the members of a division are of equal value to the division chief
B. *good*; dissatisfied members will probably be more productive elsewhere
C. *poor*; the division chief has abdicated his responsibility to carry out the order given to him
D. *good*; morale among remaining staff is likely to improve in a more cohesive framework

39. Suppose one of the volunteers is a recently appointed employee who has completed his probationary period acceptably, but whose attitude toward division operations and agency administration tends to be rather negative and sometimes even abrasive. Because of his lack of commitment to the division, his transfer is recommended. 39.___
If the transfer is approved, the division chief should, prior to the transfer,
A. discuss with the staff the importance of commitment to the work of the agency and its relationship with job satisfaction
B. refrain from any discussion of attitude with the employee
C. discuss with the employee his concern about the employee's attitude
D. avoid mention of attitude in the evaluation appraisal prepared for the receiving division chief

40. It is time to make position classification a real help to line officials in defining programs and objectives and structuring tasks to meet those objectives, rather than continuing to act as a post auditor and controller. 40.___
Of the following, the statement which BEST reflects the sense of this passage is that
A. post audit and control procedures should be related to the prior processes of objectives and goals determination
B. position classification should be part of management decisions rather than an evaluation of them

C. program definition requires prior determination of position characteristics and performance factors to facilitate management program decisions
D. primary responsibility for position classification and grade or level allocation is that of line management, not that of the classification specialist

41. Pencil and paper objective testing procedures have tremendous advantages of quantification and empiricism. They are economical in production and use. But the procedures have a great disadvantage in that they are designed primarily for statistical prediction. 41.___
A conclusion that is MOST consistent with the above statement is that
A. statistical prediction becomes meaningless if the applicants tested constitute a stratified sample and not a representative sample of the population
B. predictions of adequate performance by any one group of successful applicants will follow the normal curve
C. if the group is small, statistical indices cannot have high validity
D. such test procedures cannot predict the job success or failure of a specific applicant

42. It has been stated that in the public service, the use of written tests is more appropriate for selecting from among those outside the organization than from those within the organization. 42.___
This is so since
A. written tests serve to reduce the number of final competitors to manageable proportions
B. vouchering of prospective employees from outside the organization is deemed to be invalid and not reliable
C. written tests are in effect substitutes for direct observation on the job
D. testing outside applicants for aptitude and achievement has served a useful purpose in the elimination of extraneous prejudicial factors in the selection process

43. The *Test Validation Board* is a recent innovation. 43.___
The MAJOR purpose of this board is to review
A. and approve questions to be used before the written test is held
B. and approve the test questions and the proposed key answers immediately after the test is held
C. the test items and protests and then establish the final key answers
D. the test items and protests and then recommend adoption of a final rating key

44. *Brainstorming* sessions include each of the following EXCEPT
   A. free-wheeling or wild ideas
   B. criticism of any idea
   C. great quantities of ideas
   D. combining or building on ideas

44.____

45. It has been ascertained that a certain top-level position should NOT be placed in the competitive class.
What determines whether the new position should be placed in the non-competitive class rather than in the exempt class?
   A. Subordinate positions are in the competitive class.
   B. An executive in a specific field is needed.
   C. The position can be subjected to examination.
   D. The position is policy making.

45.____

46. Personnel practice in most governmental organizations provides that a new employee must serve a probationary period generally not to exceed six months. During this period, he is to be given special attention in such matters as instruction, indoctrination, and general adjustment to his job. The theory behind this practice is that this period is the last phase of the testing process, but the consensus is that the probationary period is not living up to its possibilities as a testing opportunity.
The MAJOR reason for this opinion is that the
   A. techniques used by personnel practitioners to encourage supervisors to pass objective judgments on probationers are not effective
   B. probationary period is too short and marginal employees can maintain their best behavior for this length of time
   C. supervisors are not living up to their obligation to conduct vigorous probationary appraisals
   D. supervisors try to avoid making unpleasant personal judgments about their employees

46.____

47. Plans were recently announced to require one year of college for entrance into the police service and eventually a college degree for promotion in the police force.
Of the following, the one that will NOT present problems in implementing these plans is
   A. changing the Civil Service requirements for entrance or promotion
   B. overcoming police union objections to the promotion requirements
   C. providing sufficient time for affected individuals to meet these educational requirements
   D. retaining college graduates in the police service over a period of years

47.____

Questions 48-50.

DIRECTIONS: Answer Questions 48 through 50 on the basis of the following paragraph.

The increase in the extent to which each individual is personally responsible to others is most noticeable in a large bureaucracy. No one person 'decides' anything; each decision of any importance is the product of an intricate process of brokerage involving individuals inside and outside the organization who feel some reason to be affected by the decision, or who have special knowledge to contribute to it. The more varied the organization's constituency, the more outside "veto-groups" will need to be taken into account. But even if no outside consultations were involved, sheer size would produce a complex process of decision. For a large organization is a deliberately created system of tensions into which each individual is expected to bring work-ways, viewpoints, and outside relationships markedly different from those of his colleagues. It is the administrator's task to draw from these disparate forces the elements of wise action from day to day, consistent with the purposes of the organization as a whole.

48. This passage is ESSENTIALLY a description of decision-making as 48.___
   A. an organization process
   B. the key responsibility of the administrator
   C. the one best position among many
   D. a complex of individual decisions

49. Which one of the following statements BEST describes the responsibilities of an administrator? 49.___
He
   A. modifies decisions and goals in accordance with pressures from within and outside the organization
   B. creates problem-solving mechanisms that rely on the varied interests of his staff and *veto-groups*
   C. makes determinations that will lead to attainment of his agency's objectives
   D. obtains agreement among varying viewpoints and interests

50. In the context of the operations of a central public personnel agency, a *veto-group* would LEAST likely consist of 50.___
   A. employee organizations
   B. professional personnel societies
   C. using agencies
   D. civil service newspapers

KEY (CORRECT ANSWERS)

1. A	11. C	21. C	31. D	41. D
2. A	12. D	22. B	32. D	42. C
3. D	13. A	23. A	33. D	43. D
4. A	14. C	24. A	34. A	44. B
5. B	15. B	25. D	35. C	45. B
6. C	16. A	26. B	36. B	46. C
7. B	17. C	27. C	37. A	47. C
8. C	18. B	28. D	38. A	48. A
9. A	19. A	29. B	39. C	49. C
10. B	20. D	30. A	40. B	50. B

TEST 2

DIRECTIONS: Each question or incomplete statement is followed by several suggested answers or completions. Select the one that BEST answers the question or completes the statement. *PRINT THE LETTER OF THE CORRECT ANSWER IN THE SPACE AT THE RIGHT.*

1. The definition of merit system as it pertains to the public service is that a person's worth to the organization is the factor governing both his entrance and upward mobility within that service. The main ingredient used to accomplish entrance and mobility has been competition based on relative qualifications of candidates. 1.___
   The burgeoning demands of new occupations and critical social and economic urgencies in the public service make it imperative that now
   A. greater emphasis be placed on the intellectual and technical capacities of applicants in order to improve the high standards achieved by some professionals
   B. current methods be strengthened in order to make them more valid and reliable indicators among applicants for government positions
   C. public personnel officials work more closely with representatives of the various professions and occupations to establish more equitable minimum standards in order to improve the quality of its practitioners
   D. the system adapt to the new changes by establishing alternative methods more suitable to current needs

2. Civil service systems need to be reexamined from time to time to determine whether they are correctly fulfilling stated merit obligations. Frequently, inspection determines that what was once a valid practice...has ceased to be an effective instrument and has become, instead, an unrealistic barrier to the implementation of merit principles. 2.___
   Which one of the following practices would be considered to be such an unrealistic barrier?
   A. Disqualifying candidates with poor work history for positions involving the operation of trains or buses
   B. Disqualifying candidates for police work who have records of serious arrests
   C. Requiring a degree or license for medical, scientific, and professional positions
   D. Requiring a high school diploma for custodial, maintenance, and service positions

3. It is generally accepted that work attitudes and interpersonal relationships contribute at least as much as knowledge and ability to job performance. Several personality measuring and appraisal devices have been found useful in predicting personality and work attitudes. 3.___

A MAJOR drawback in their use in competitive selection, however, is the
- A. *fakeability* of responses possible in such selection situations
- B. cost of the materials and their interpretation
- C. inability of these measures to predict actual job performance
- D. lack of reviewability of these devices

4. Human Relations School discoveries having a major impact on modern personnel practices include all of the following EXCEPT that 4.___
   - A. social as well as physical capacity determines the amount of work an employee does
   - B. non-economic rewards play a central role in employee motivation
   - C. the higher the degree of specialization, the more efficient the division of labor
   - D. workers react to management as members of groups rather than as individuals

5. Studies of the relationship between creativity and intelligence indicate that creativity 5.___
   - A. is one of several special intelligence factors
   - B. consists primarily of general intelligence as measured by standardized tests
   - C. involves non-intellective factors as well as minimums of intelligence
   - D. relates more directly to quantitative than to verbal aptitudes and skills

6. Strategies of data collection applicable to personnel work can be grouped into two broad categories: the mechanical method in which data be collected according to pre-established guidelines, rules, or procedures, and the clinical method in which the manner of data collection may differ from candidate to candidate at the discretion of the professional person collecting it. 6.___
   An argument that has proved VALID in support of the clinical method is that
   - A. no sound basis exists for writing any single set of rules for collecting data
   - B. no known mechanical procedure can fully anticipate all potentially relevant data
   - C. mechanical processes stress the use of techniques such as synthetic validation
   - D. mechanical methods are inadequate for formulating optimal individualized prediction rules

7. Which one of the following actions appears LEAST mandated by the Griggs vs. Duke Power Company decision of the U.S. Supreme Court on discriminatory employment practice? 7.___
   - A. Study of certification and appointment policies and procedures
   - B. Determination of job performance standards as related to successful performance

C. Review of personal history forms, applications, and interviews involved in employment procedures
D. Test validation by correlation of individual test items with total test scores

8. In decision-making terminology, the type of action taken on a problem when the decision-maker finds that he cannot do anything to eliminate the cause is MOST often called ____ action. 8.___
A. corrective
B. adaptive
C. stopgap
D. interim

9. The Intergovernmental Personnel Act became law recently. This Act does NOT provide for 9.___
A. temporary assignment of personnel between governmental jurisdiction
B. grants for improving personnel administration and training
C. interstate compacts for personnel and training activities
D. a National Advisory Council to study federal personnel administration and make recommendations to the President and Congress

10. Following are three kinds of performance tests for which arrangements might be made to give the candidates a pre-test warm-up period: 10.___
I. typing
II. truck driving
III. stenography
Which one of the following choices lists all of the above tests that should be preceded by a warm-up session?
A. I, III
B. II *only*
C. I, II, III
D. None of the above

Questions 11-12.

DIRECTIONS: Answer Questions 11 and 12 on the basis of the following paragraph.

Your role as human resources utilization experts is to submit your techniques to operating administrators, for the program must in reality be theirs, not yours. We in personnel have been guilty of encouraging operating executives to believe that these important matters affecting their employees are personnel department matters, not management matters. We should hardly be surprised, as a consequence, to find these executives playing down the role of personnel and finding personnel "routines" a nuisance, for these are not in the mainstream of managing the enterprise -- or so we have encouraged them to believe.

11. The BEST of the following interpretations of the above paragraph is that 11.___
A. personnel people have been guilty of *passing the buck* on personnel functions
B. operating officials have difficulty understanding personnel techniques

C. personnel employees have tended to usurp some functions rightfully belonging to management
D. matters affecting employees should be handled by the personnel department

12. The BEST of the following interpretations of the above paragraph is that 12.____
A. personnel departments have aided and abetted the formulation of negative attitudes on the part of management
B. personnel people are labor relations experts and should carry out these duties
C. personnel activities are not really the responsibility of management
D. management is now being encouraged by personnel experts to assume some responsibility for personnel functions

13. Employee training can be described BEST as a process that 13.____
A. increases retention of skills
B. changes employees' knowledge, skills, or attitudes
C. improves the work methods used
D. improves the work environment

14. With respect to the use of on-the-job training methods, the theory is that it is possible to create maximally favorable conditions for learning while on the job. In actual practice, it has been found that these favorable conditions are difficult to achieve. 14.____
The MAIN reason militating against such ideal conditions is that
A. the primary function on the job is production, and training must, therefore, take second place
B. an adequate number of skilled and knowledgeable employees is usually not available to engage in effective person-to-person training
C. expensive equipment and work space are tied up during training, which is not advantageous to establishing good rapport between trainer and trainee
D. an appraisal of trainee learning under pressure of job demands is not conducive to showing the trainee the reasons for his mistakes

15. In most major studies directed toward identification of productive scientific personnel, the MOST effective predictor has been 15.____
A. biographical information
B. motivational analysis
C. tests of ideational flexibility
D. high-level reasoning tests

16. Because interviewing is a difficult art, MOST personnel people who conduct interviews 16.____
A. break the interview into specific units with pauses in between
B. remain fairly constant in the technique they use despite differences of purpose and persons interviewed

C. utilize non-directive techniques during their first few years of interviewing
D. vary their style and technique in accordance with the purpose of the interview and the personality of the persons interviewed

17. When using the *in-basket* technique, it is NOT possible to obtain measures of the 17.___
A. amount of work done in a given time
B. extent to which the candidate seeks guidance before making decisions
C. proportion of decisions that lead to actual cost savings
D. proportion of work time devoted to prepatory activities

18. The MOST appropriate people to develop the definition for specific classes of positions in order that they may serve as useful criteria for allocating positions to classes are the 18.___
A. personnel experts in the area of job evaluation
B. program practitioners
C. job analysts working within other occupations under study
D. organization and methods analysts

19. By its very nature and in order to operate effectively, a job classification system which groups jobs into broad occupational categories and then subdivides them into levels of difficulty and responsibility requires 19.___
A. the upgrading of positions in order to raise the pay rates of incumbents
B. a process in which lengthy job descriptions covering the allocation criteria are prerequisites
C. a certain amount of central control
D. the transfer of classification authority from an *inside-track priesthood* to the operating official

20. A plan of classifying positions based on duties and responsibilities is not the same thing as a pay plan. Although the classification arrangement may be a vital element upon which a compensation structure is based and administered, there are differences between the two plans. The MAJOR distinction between these plans can be illustrated best by the fact that 20.___
A. a uniform accounting system requires a uniform job terminology, which can be accomplished best by a classification plan
B. the compensation plan can be changed without affecting the classification plan, and classes of positions can be rearranged on a pay schedule without changing the schedule
C. job evaluation results in a common understanding of the job for which a rate is being set and for job-to-job comparison
D. the classification principle of *equal pay for equal work* was instrumental in evolving pay reform

21. By stretching higher grade duties over as many jobs as possible, the position classifier makes for 21.___
   A. economy
   B. more effective performance
   C. effective use of the labor market
   D. higher operational costs

22. Contemporary information about what people want that is pertinent to potential entrants to the public service labor market indicates that a MAJOR want is 22.___
   A. more time for play and less time for work
   B. more personal privacy and fewer creature comforts
   C. more employee relationships and less organizational hierarchy
   D. more political participation and less partisan neutrality

23. An occupational rather than an organizational commitment to personnel administration as a professional field is MOST likely to prevail among personnel workers who perceive their work as part of a function that is 23.___
   A. designed to serve the employees of their agency
   B. dominated by necessary but uninteresting tasks
   C. dedicated to obtaining compliance with the law
   D. devoted to the human problems of organizations

24. The FIRST major strike by city employees which tested the Condon-Wadlin Act was by employees of the 24.___
   A. Sanitation Department B. Police Department
   C. Fire Department D. Department of Welfare

25. In the aftermath of the city transit strike of 1966, study groups were appointed to recommend ways in which such strikes could be avoided. 25.___
The recommendations made at that time by the Governor's Committee and the American Arbitration Association were especially significant in that they both
   A. included machinery for the settlement of labor disputes which was to be set up outside the regular civil service establishment
   B. advocated the retention of the legal prohibition against strikes by public employees
   C. agreed to imposition of heavy fines on the union in case of a strike
   D. opted for repeal of the section in the Condon-Wadlin Act which prohibited strikes

26. Of the following, which country was the pioneer in employee-management relationships within the public service? 26.___
   A. Canada B. France C. Australia D. Mexico

27. There are notable similarities and differences between collective bargaining in industry and government. 27.___
In which of the following areas are the similarities GREATEST?
   A. Negotiable subjects B. Bargaining processes
   C. Mediation and arbitration D. Strikes

28. Traditionally, white-collar and professional workers resisted unionization both in government and in industry. This attitude has changed drastically among these workers since the late 1950's, however, particularly among public employees.
The BASIC cause behind this change among public employees was that
   A. organized labor trained its big union recruitment guns on organizing these workers in the face of the dwindling proportion of blue-collar people in the labor force
   B. these employees generally identified with middle-class America, which had now become union-oriented
   C. they felt deep frustration with the authoritarianism of public administrators who believed that the *merit system* process gave the employee all the protection he needed
   D. the continual upward spiral of inflation resulted in making these workers among those deemed economically disadvantaged and necessitated their joining in unions for their own protection

28.___

29. Union efforts to improve retirement benefits for public employees have caused concern in the State legislature. Recently, a special legislative committee was ordered to determine whether retirement benefits should remain a subject for collective bargaining or whether they should be regulated by
   A. a bipartisan pension commission
   B. a board designated by management and labor
   C. large commercial insurance carriers
   D. the State Insurance Fund

29.___

30. The performance of personnel functions which are part of a comprehensive and integrated program of personnel management is conditioned significantly by personnel policies. Which one of the following is the LEAST valid criterion of what positive policies can accomplish?
   A. Functions are governed by rules which permit their being performed in line with the desired goals of the organization.
   B. Guidance for executives restrains them from mishandling the specified functions with which they have been entrusted.
   C. Standard decisions make it unnecessary for subordinates to ask their supervisors how given problems should be handled.
   D. Goals are enunciated for the purpose of selecting candidates best equipped to prove successful in the particular organizational milieu.

30.___

31. The GREATEST handicap of personnel systems which are predicated on the *corps of people* concept rather than on job analysis is lack of facility for
   A. conducting program evaluation studies
   B. developing sound programs for the direction and control of productivity

31.___

C. manpower planning
D. determining the limits of authority and responsibility among managerial personnel

32. It is an anomaly that one of the greatest threats to maintaining classification plans adequately is slowness in adjusting salaries to keep up with the changing labor market. Thus, distortions of many classification plans occur.
This is MAINLY due to
A. pressure from management officials to upgrade employees who have not received salary range increases
B. inability to maintain an adequate file of pertinent pay data
C. conflict in the pay philosophy between maintaining external alignment and comparability with union rates
D. difficulty in distinguishing between the pay program and the fringe benefit package

32.___

33. A personnel agency charged with identifying candidates with the kind of creative talent that can be used in an organizational setting should look for a high degree of certain attributes among the candidate population.
Below are listed four characteristics which may qualify as desirable attributes for the purpose indicated:
I. Self-confidence
II. Social conformity
III. Mobility aspirations
IV. Job involvement

Which of the following choices lists ALL of the above attributes which the personnel agency should look for?
A. I, II, IV
B. I, III, IV
C. II, III, IV
D. III, IV

33.___

34. With regard to educational standards for selection purposes, the U.S. Supreme Court has held that such requirements should be
A. eliminated in most cases
B. related to job success
C. maintained whenever possible
D. reduced as far as possible

34.___

35. In surveying job series which would be most conducive to job restructuring, most attention has focused on P, T, and M positions.
The benefits claimed for job restructuring include all of the following EXCEPT
A. creating more interesting and challenging P, T, and M jobs
B. increasing promotional opportunities for P, T, and M employees
C. providing more job opportunities for the lesser skilled
D. creating new promotional opportunities for those in low-skill or dead-end jobs

35.___

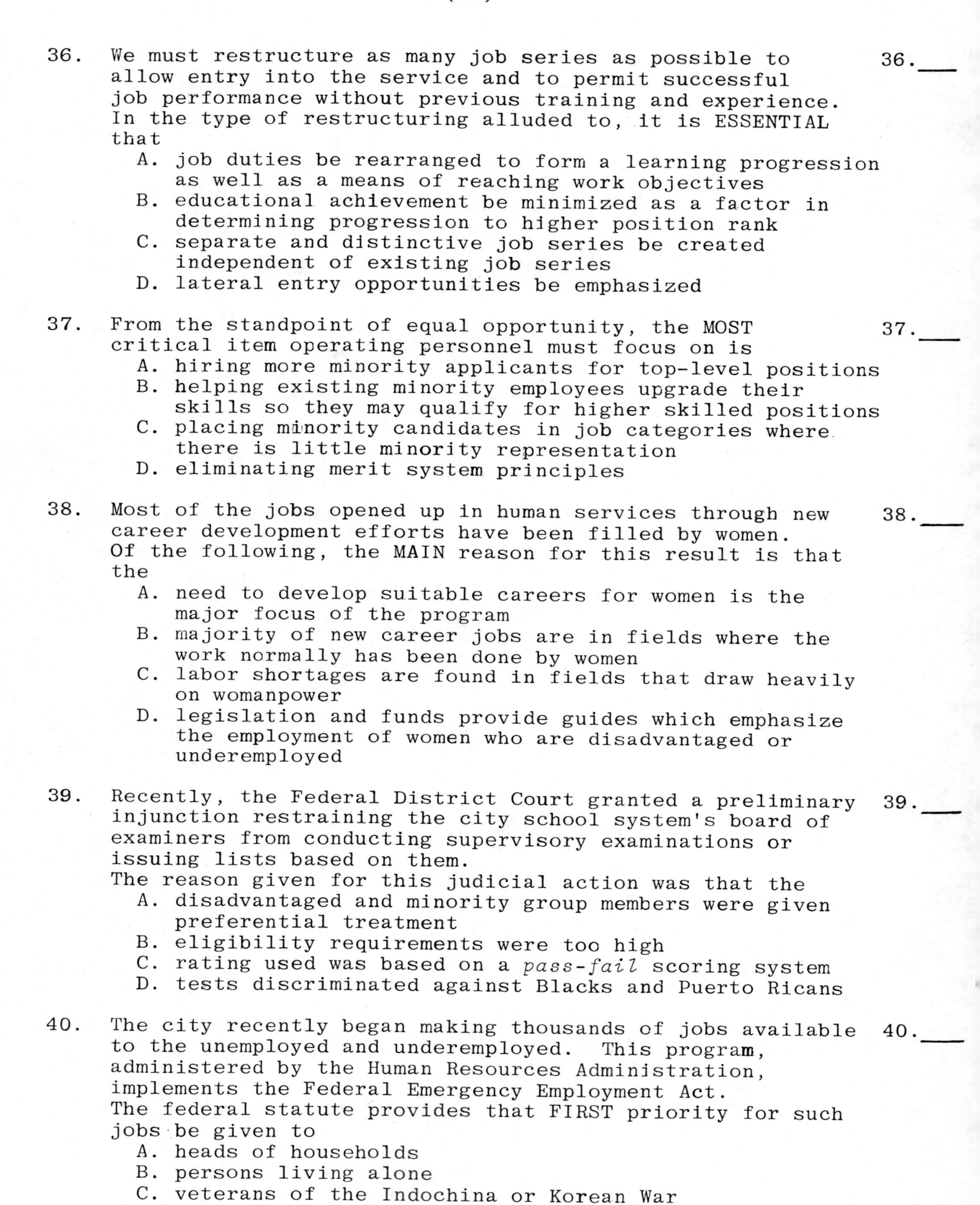

36. We must restructure as many job series as possible to allow entry into the service and to permit successful job performance without previous training and experience. In the type of restructuring alluded to, it is ESSENTIAL that 36.___
   A. job duties be rearranged to form a learning progression as well as a means of reaching work objectives
   B. educational achievement be minimized as a factor in determining progression to higher position rank
   C. separate and distinctive job series be created independent of existing job series
   D. lateral entry opportunities be emphasized

37. From the standpoint of equal opportunity, the MOST critical item operating personnel must focus on is 37.___
   A. hiring more minority applicants for top-level positions
   B. helping existing minority employees upgrade their skills so they may qualify for higher skilled positions
   C. placing minority candidates in job categories where there is little minority representation
   D. eliminating merit system principles

38. Most of the jobs opened up in human services through new career development efforts have been filled by women. Of the following, the MAIN reason for this result is that the 38.___
   A. need to develop suitable careers for women is the major focus of the program
   B. majority of new career jobs are in fields where the work normally has been done by women
   C. labor shortages are found in fields that draw heavily on womanpower
   D. legislation and funds provide guides which emphasize the employment of women who are disadvantaged or underemployed

39. Recently, the Federal District Court granted a preliminary injunction restraining the city school system's board of examiners from conducting supervisory examinations or issuing lists based on them. The reason given for this judicial action was that the 39.___
   A. disadvantaged and minority group members were given preferential treatment
   B. eligibility requirements were too high
   C. rating used was based on a *pass-fail* scoring system
   D. tests discriminated against Blacks and Puerto Ricans

40. The city recently began making thousands of jobs available to the unemployed and underemployed. This program, administered by the Human Resources Administration, implements the Federal Emergency Employment Act. The federal statute provides that FIRST priority for such jobs be given to 40.___
   A. heads of households
   B. persons living alone
   C. veterans of the Indochina or Korean War
   D. youths entering the labor market

41. According to the Equal Employment Opportunity Act of 1966, a covered employer may NOT 41.___
   A. discriminate against an individual because he is a member of the Communist Party in the United States
   B. indicate preference for or limitation to national origin in printing a notice or advertisement for employment
   C. employ only members of a certain religion if the employer is an educational institution owned or supported by that religion
   D. apply different pay scales, conditions, or facilities of employment according to the location of various plants or facilities

42. Data received by the Equal Employment Opportunity Commission from firms employing 100 or more people suggest that emphasis in the area of equal opportunity has shifted from one of detection of conscious discrimination to one of 42.___
   A. human resources utilization
   B. passive resistance
   C. unconscious discrimination
   D. education

43. According to surveys pertaining to equal employment opportunities, available information indicates that discriminatory patterns in job placement of minority group members is 43.___
   A. higher in craft unions than in industrial unions
   B. greater in the East than in the West
   C. higher in new plants than in old plants
   D. higher among young executives than among old executives

44. The area of criticism on which Congress concentrated its attention in its recent investigations of testing was 44.___
   A. cultural bias
   B. depersonalization of the individual
   C. increase in *meritocracy*
   D. invasion of privacy

45. If accepted criteria of a profession are applied, which of the following work groupings ranks LOWEST in the distinctiveness of its character as a profession? 45.___
   A. Social service or community work
   B. Managerial or administrative work
   C. Health or health services work
   D. Teaching or educational work

46. Surveys of factors contributing to job satisfaction indicate, according to employees, that the factor having HIGHEST priority among those listed is 46.___
   A. opportunity for advancement
   B. good pay schedules
   C. concern for training employees for better job performance
   D. good work environment

47. Job enrichment is intended to increase employee motivation and interest by increasing the accountability of employees for their work, by introducing more complex tasks, and by granting authority to make job decisions.
A MAJOR hazard that may result from application of such restructuring is to
   A. increase complaints of work pressure
   B. reduce the effectiveness of task specialization
   C. stimulate demand for salary increases
   D. limit the status of the immediate supervisor

47.___

48. Which of the following statements concerning performance appraisal systems is NOT correct?
They
   A. require line management participation
   B. provide for periodic discussions of performance between the supervisor and the employee
   C. are used primarily to uncover employee weaknesses
   D. require supervisor training to assure uniform appraisals

48.___

49. In the forced-choice technique of performance evaluation, the rater is forced to judge which of several alternative statements is most descriptive of an employee's performance. It forces the rater to discriminate on the basis of concrete aspects of a subordinate's work behavior rather than to rely on an impression of his total worth.
The one of the following which is NOT considered a value of this technique is that it
   A. increases rater ability to produce a desired outcome
   B. is relatively free of the usual pile-up at the top of the scale
   C. tends to minimize subjective elements
   D. produces results that correlate positively with other variables associated with effective job performance

49.___

50. Of the following, the one which is NOT an advantage of the proper delegation of work by a manager is that it
   A. increases planning time
   B. relieves the tension of seeing to details
   C. increases the manager's familiarity with routine work
   D. increases understanding of the responsibilities of subordinates

50.___

KEY (CORRECT ANSWERS)

1. D	11. C	21. D	31. C	41. B
2. D	12. A	22. C	32. A	42. A
3. A	13. B	23. D	33. B	43. A
4. C	14. A	24. D	34. B	44. D
5. C	15. D	25. A	35. B	45. B
6. B	16. B	26. A	36. A	46. A
7. D	17. C	27. B	37. B	47. D
8. B	18. A	28. C	38. B	48. C
9. D	19. C	29. A	39. D	49. A
10. C	20. B	30. D	40. C	50. C

EXAMINATION SECTION

DIRECTIONS: Each question or incomplete statement is followed by several suggested answers or completions. Select the one that BEST answers the question or completes the statement. *PRINT THE LETTER OF THE CORRECT ANSWER IN THE SPACE AT THE RIGHT.*

1. The CHIEF assumption underlying the provisions for a salary range with a minimum, a maximum, and intervening steps for each class in the compensation plans of MOST public agencies is that 1.___
   A. the granting of periodic increments to employees encourages staff stability at the lowest possible cost
   B. job offers made at a step higher than the minimum of a salary range are a positive aid to recruitment
   C. automatic salary increments provide an incentive to employees to improve their job performances from year to year
   D. an employee's value to his employer tends to increase with the passage of time

2. Selection of candidates for employment on the basis of aptitude test results is made on the assumption that the candidates making the highest test scores 2.___
   A. possess the most knowledge about the job for which they were tested
   B. will need a minimum amount of training on the job for which they were tested
   C. will be the most satisfactory employees after they have received training
   D. are those who will have the highest interest in succeeding on the job for which they were tested

3. In position classification, the one of the following factors which is of LEAST importance in classifying a clerical position is the 3.___
   A. degree of supervision under which the work of the position is performed
   B. amount of supervision exercised over other positions
   C. training and experience of the incumbent of the position
   D. extent to which independent judgment must be exercised in performing the duties of the position

4. The position classifying bureau of the central personnel agency in a public jurisdiction is normally NOT responsible for 4.___
   A. allocating individual positions to classes
   B. assigning titles to classes of positions
   C. establishing minimum qualifications for positions
   D. determining which positions are necessary

5. The one of the following which is generally considered to be an ESSENTIAL element in the process of classifying a position in a civil service system is the 5.____
   A. comparison of the position with similar and related positions
   B. evaluation of the skill with which the duties of the position are being performed
   C. number of positions similar to the position being classified
   D. determination of the salary being paid for the position

6. Of the following, the LEAST important objective of a modern service rating system which is applied to civil service positions is to 6.____
   A. validate selection procedures
   B. improve the quality of supervision
   C. furnish a basis for the construction of a position classification plan
   D. foster the development of good employee performance

7. Some public agencies conduct exit interviews with employees who quit their jobs. 7.____
   The one of the following which is generally considered to be the CHIEF value to a public agency of such an interview is in
   A. ascertaining from the employee the reasons why he is leaving his job
   B. obtaining reliable information on the employee's work history with the agency
   C. persuading the employee to reconsider his decision to quit
   D. giving the employee a final evaluation of his work performance

8. The rate of labor turnover in an organization may be arrived at by dividing the total number of separations from the organization in a given period by the average number of workers employed in the same period. In arriving at the rate, it is assumed that those separated are replaced. 8.____
   If the rate of turnover is excessively low in comparison with other similar organizations, it USUALLY indicates that
   A. the organization is stagnant
   B. promotions within the organization are made frequently
   C. the organization's recruitment policies have been ineffective
   D. suitable workers are in short supply

9. Of the following aspects of a training program for supervisory personnel in a public agency, the aspect for which it is usually the MOST difficult to develop adequate information is the 9.____
   A. determination of the training needs of the supervisory personnel in the agency
   B. establishment of the objectives of the program
   C. selection of suitable training methods for the program
   D. evaluation of the effectiveness of the training program

10. You are conducting a training conference for new supervisors on supervisory techniques and problems. When one of the participants in the conference proposes what you consider to be an unsatisfactory solution for the problem under discussion, none of the other participants questions the solution or offers an alternate solution. For you to tell the group why the solution is unsatisfactory would be 10.___
   A. *desirable* chiefly because satisfactory rather than unsatisfactory solutions to the problems should be stressed in the conference
   B. *undesirable* chiefly because the participants themselves should be stimulated to present reasons why the proposed solution is unsatisfactory
   C. *desirable* chiefly because you, as the conference leader, should guide the participants in solving conference problems
   D. *undesirable* chiefly because the proposed unsatisfactory solution may be useful in illustrating the advantages of a satisfactory solution

11. It is generally BEST that the greater part of in-service training for the operating employees of an agency in a public jurisdiction be given by 11.___
   A. a team of trainers from the central personnel agency of the jurisdiction
   B. training specialists on the staff of the personnel unit of the agency
   C. a team of teachers from the public school system of the jurisdiction
   D. members of the regular supervisory force of the agency

12. You are responsible for training a number of your subordinates to handle some complicated procedures which your unit will adopt after the training has been completed. If approximately 30 hours of training are required and you can arrange the training sessions during working hours as you see fit, learning would ordinarily be BEST effected if you scheduled the trainees to devote ____ to the training until it is completed. 12.___
   A. a half day each week B. one full day each week
   C. a half day every day D. full time

13. Assume that you are giving a lecture for the purpose of explaining a new procedure. You find that the employees attending the lecture are asking many questions on the material as you present it. Consequently, you realize that you will be unable to cover all of the material you had intended to cover, and that a second lecture will be necessary. In this situation, the MOST advisable course of action for you to take would be to 13.___
   A. answer the questions on the new procedure as they arise

B. answer the questions that can be answered quickly and ask the employees to reserve questions requiring lengthier answers for the second lecture
C. suggest that further questions be withheld until the second lecture so that you can cover as much of the remaining material as possible
D. refer the questions back to the employees asking them

14. As a supervisor, you are conducting a training conference dealing with administrative principles and practices. One of the members of the conference, Mr. Smith, makes a factual statement which you know to be incorrect and which may hinder the development of the discussion. None of the other members attempts to correct Mr. Smith or to question him on what he has said, although until this point, the members have participated actively in the discussions.
In this situation, the MOST advisable course of action for you to take would be to
A. proceed with the discussion without commenting on Mr. Smith's statement
B. correct the statement that Mr. Smith has made
C. emphasize that the material discussed at the conference is to serve only as a guide for handling actual work situations
D. urge the members to decide for themselves whether or not to accept factual statements made at the conference

14.___

15. With the wholehearted support of top management, the training bureau of a public agency schedules a series of training conferences for all the supervisory and administrative employees in order to alter their approaches to the problems arising from the interaction of supervisors and subordinates. During the conferences, the participants discuss solutions to typical problems of this type and become conscious of the principles underlying these solutions. After the series of conferences is concluded, it is found that the first-line supervisors are not applying the principles to the problems they are encountering on the job.
Of the following, the MOST likely reason why these supervisors are not putting the principles into practice is that
A. the training conferences have not changed the attitudes of these supervisors
B. these supervisors are reluctant to put into practice methods with which their subordinates are unfamiliar
C. the conference method is not suitable for human relations training
D. the principles which were covered in the conferences are not suitable for solving actual work problems

15.___

16. Assume that you are the leader of a training conference dealing with supervisory techniques and problems. One of the problems being discussed is one with which you have had no experience, but two of the participants have had considerable experience with it. These two participants carry on an extended discussion of the problem in light of their experiences, and it is obvious from their discussion that they understand the problem thoroughly. It is also obvious that the other participants in the conference are very much interested in the discussion and are taking notes on the material presented.
For you to permit the two participants to continue until the amount of time allowed for discussion of the problem has been exhausted would be — 16.___
   A. *desirable* chiefly because their discussion, which is based on actual work experience, may be more meaningful to the other participants than would a discussion which is not based on work experience
   B. *undesirable* chiefly because they are discussing the material only in the light of their own experiences rather than in general terms
   C. *desirable* chiefly because the introduction of the material by two of the participants themselves may put the other participants at ease
   D. *undesirable* chiefly because the other participants are not joining in the discussion of the problem

17. You are a supervisor in charge of a unit of clerical employees. One of your subordinates, Mr. Smith, has not seemed to be his usual self in the past several weeks, but rather has seemed to be disturbed. In addition, he has not been producing his usual quantity of work and has been provoking arguments with his colleagues. He approaches you and asks if he may discuss with you a problem which he believes has been affecting his work. As Mr. Smith begins to discuss the problem, you immediately realize that, although it may be disturbing to him, it is really a trivial matter.
Of the following, the FIRST step that you should take in this situation is to — 17.___
   A. permit Mr. Smith to continue to describe his problem, interrupting him only when clarification of a point is needed
   B. tell Mr. Smith that his becoming unduly upset about the problem will not help to solve it
   C. point out that you and your subordinates have faced more serious problems and that this one is a relatively minor matter
   D. suggest that the problem should be solved before it develops into a serious matter

18. A line supervisor can play an important role in helping his subordinates to make healthy mental, emotional, and social adjustments.
The one of the following which would NOT be considered to be a part of the supervisor's role in helping his subordinates to make these adjustments is to — 18.___

A. ascertain which subordinates are likely to develop maladjustments
B. recognize indications of these types of maladjustments
C. refer subordinates displaying signs of maladjustments that he cannot handle to specialists for assistance
D. create a work environment that will tend to minimize his subordinates' preoccupations with personal problems

19. One of the principal duties of the management in a public agency is to secure the most effective utilization of personnel. 19.___
The one of the following which would contribute LEAST to effective utilization and development of personnel in a public agency is
A. the use of training programs designed to prepare employees for future tasks
B. a comprehensive list of skills and abilities needed to perform the work of the agency effectively
C. a systematic effort to discover employees of high potential and to develop them for future responsibilities
D. the assignment of employees to duties which require the maximum use of their abilities

20. During a training session for new employees, an employee becomes upset because he is unable to solve a problem presented to him by the instructor. 20.___
Of the following actions which the instructor could take, the one which would be MOST likely to dispel the employee's emotional state is to
A. give him a different type of problem which he may be able to solve
B. minimize the importance of finding a solution to the problem and proceed to the next topic
C. encourage the other participants to contribute to the solution
D. provide him with hints which would enable him to solve the problem

21. Studies in human behavior have shown that an employee in a work group who is capable of producing substantially more work than is being produced by the average of the group GENERALLY will 21.___
A. tend to produce substantially more work than is produced by the average member of the group
B. attempt to become the informal leader of the group
C. tend to produce less work than he is capable of producing
D. attempt to influence the other members of the group to increase their production

22. Studies of organizations show that formal employee participation in the formulation of work policies before they are put into effect is MOST likely to result in a(n) 22.____
   A. reduction in the length of time required to formulate the policies
   B. increase in the number of employees affected by the policies
   C. reduction in the length of time required to implement the policies
   D. increase in the number of policies formulated within the organization

23. No matter how elaborate a formal system of communication is in an organization, the system will always be supplemented by informal channels of communication, such as the *grapevine*. Although such informal channels of communication are usually not highly regarded, they sometimes are of value to an organization. 23.____
Of the following, the CHIEF value of informal channels of communication is that they serve to
   A. transmit information that management has neglected to send through the formal system of communication
   B. confirm information that has already been received through the formal system of communication
   C. hinder the formation of employee cliques in the organization
   D. revise information sent through the formal system of communication

24. The one of the following which is generally considered to be the MOST important advantage of the written questionnaire method of obtaining information is that this method 24.____
   A. assures accuracy of response greater than that obtained from other methods
   B. gives the persons to whom the questionnaire is sent the opportunity to express their opinions and feelings
   C. makes it possible to obtain the responses of many persons at small cost
   D. permits errors in the information obtained to be corrected easily when they are discovered

25. In collecting objective data for the evaluation of procedures which are used in his agency, an administrator should, in every case, be careful 25.____
   A. to take an equal number of measurements from each source of information
   B. not to allow his beliefs about the values of the procedures to influence the choice of data
   C. to apply statistical methods continuously to the data as they are gathered to assure maximum accuracy
   D. not to accept data which are inconsistent with the general trend established by verified data

26. Assume that the law enforcement division in a public jurisdiction employs only males who are 5 feet 8 inches or taller. 26.___
To expect the heights of these employees to be normally distributed is UNJUSTIFIED primarily because
   A. the distribution of a random sample is not usually the same as the distribution of the population from which the sample was drawn
   B. no maximum height requirement has been established
   C. height is a characteristic which is not normally distributed in the general population of males
   D. the employees are not a representative sample of the general population of males

Questions 27-30.

DIRECTIONS: Questions 27 through 30 are to be answered SOLELY on the basis of the information contained in the following paragraph.

A standard comprises characteristics attached to an aspect of a process or product by which it can be evaluated. Standardization is the development and adoption of standards. When they are formulated, standards are not usually the product of a single person, but represent the thoughts and ideas of a group, leavened with the knowledge and information which are currently available. Standards which do not meet certain basic requirements become a hindrance rather than an aid to progress. Standards must not only be correct, accurate, and precise in requiring no more and no less than what is needed for satisfactory results, but they must also be workable in the sense that their usefulness is not nullified by external conditions. Standards should also be acceptable to the people who use them. If they are not acceptable, they cannot be considered to be satisfactory, although they may possess all the other essential characteristics.

27. According to the above paragraph, a processing standard that requires the use of materials that cannot be procured is MOST likely to be 27.___
   A. incomplete
   B. inaccurate
   C. unworkable
   D. unacceptable

28. According to the above paragraph, the construction of standards to which the performance of job duties should conform is MOST often 28.___
   A. the work of the people responsible for seeing that the duties are properly performed
   B. accomplished by the person who is best informed about the functions involved
   C. the responsibility of the people who are to apply them
   D. attributable to the efforts of various informed persons

29. According to the above paragraph, when standards call for finer tolerances than those essential to the conduct of successful production operations, the effect of the standards on the improvement of production operations is 29.___
   A. negative
   B. nullified
   C. negligible
   D. beneficial

30. The one of the following which is the MOST suitable title for the above paragraph is 30.___
   A. The Evaluation of Formulated Standards
   B. The Attributes of Satisfactory Standards
   C. The Adoption of Acceptable Standards
   D. The Use of Process or Product Standards

Questions 31-34.

DIRECTIONS: Questions 31 through 34 are to be answered SOLELY on the basis of the information contained in the following paragraph.

Good personnel relations of an organization depend upon mutual confidence, trust, and good will. The basis of confidence is understanding. Most troubles start with people who do not understand each other. When the organization's intentions or motives are misunderstood, or when reasons for actions, practices, or policies are misconstrued, complete cooperation from individuals is not forthcoming. If management expects full cooperation from employees, it has a responsibility of sharing with them the information which is the foundation of proper understanding, confidence, and trust. Personnel management has long since outgrown the days when it was the vogue to "treat them rough and tell them nothing." Up-to-date personnel management provides all possible information about the activities, aims, and purposes of the organization. It seems altogether creditable that a desire should exist among employees for such information which the best-intentioned executive might think would not interest them and which the worst-intentioned would think was none of their business.

31. The above paragraph implies that one of the causes of the difficulty which an organization might have with its personnel relations is that its employees 31.___
   A. have not expressed interest in the activities, aims, and purposes of the organization
   B. do not believe in the good faith of the organization
   C. have not been able to give full cooperation to the organization
   D. do not recommend improvements in the practices and policies of the organization

32. According to the above paragraph, in order for an organization to have good personnel relations, it is NOT essential that 32.___
   A. employees have confidence in the organization
   B. the purposes of the organization be understood by the employees

C. employees have a desire for information about the organization
D. information about the organization be communicated to employees

33. According to the paragraph, an organization which provides full information about itself to its employees 33.____
A. understands the intentions of its employees
B. satisfies a praiseworthy desire among its employees
C. is managed by executives who have the best intentions toward its employees
D. is confident that its employees understand its motives

34. The one of the following which is the MOST suitable title for the paragraph is 34.____
A. The Foundations of Personnel Relations
B. The Consequences of Employee Misunderstanding
C. The Development of Personnel Management Practices
D. The Acceptance of Organizational Objectives

Questions 35-38.

DIRECTIONS: Questions 35 through 38 are to be answered SOLELY on the basis of the information contained in the following paragraph.

Management, which is the function of executive leadership, has as its principal phases the planning, organizing, and controlling of the activities of subordinate groups in the accomplishment of organizational objectives. Planning specifies the kind and extent of the factors, forces, and effects, and the relationships among them, that will be required for satisfactory accomplishment. The nature of the objectives and their requirements must be known before determinations can be made as to what must be done, how it must be done and why, where actions should take place, who should be responsible, and similar problems pertaining to the formulation of a plan. Organizing, which creates the conditions that must be present before the execution of the plan can be undertaken successfully, cannot be done intelligently without knowledge of the organizational objectives. Control, which has to do with the constraint and regulation of activities entering into the execution of the plan, must be exercised in accordance with the characteristics and requirements of the activities demanded by the plan.

35. The one of the following which is the MOST suitable title for the paragraph is 35.____
A. The Nature of Successful Organization
B. The Planning of Management Functions
C. The Importance of Organizational Objectives
D. The Principle Aspects of Management

36. It can be inferred from the paragraph that the one of the following functions whose existence is essential to the existence of the other three is the 36.____
A. regulation of the work needed to carry out a plan
B. understanding of what the organization intends to accomplish

C. securing of information of the factors necessary for accomplishment of objectives
D. establishment of the conditions required for successful action

37. The one of the following which would NOT be included within any of the principal phases of the function of executive leadership as defined in the paragraph is
A. determination of manpower requirements
B. procurement of required material
C. establishment of organizational objectives
D. scheduling of production

37.____

38. The conclusion which can MOST reasonably be drawn from the paragraph is that the control phase of managing is most directly concerned with the
A. influencing of policy determinations
B. administering of suggestion systems
C. acquisition of staff for the organization
D. implementation of performance standards

38.____

39. A study reveals that Miss Brown files N cards in M hours, and Miss Smith files the same number of cards in T hours. If the two employees work together, the number of hours it will take them to file N cards is
A. $\frac{N}{\frac{N}{M} + \frac{N}{T}}$
B. $\frac{N}{T + M} + \frac{2N}{MT}$
C. $N(\frac{M}{N} + \frac{N}{T})$
D. $\frac{N}{NT + MN}$

39.____

Questions 40-45.

DIRECTIONS: Questions 40 through 45 are to be answered SOLELY on the basis of the information contained in the five charts below which relate to Bureau X in a City Department. The Bureau has an office in each of the five boroughs.

NUMBER OF UNITS OF WORK PRODUCED IN THE BUREAU PER YEAR

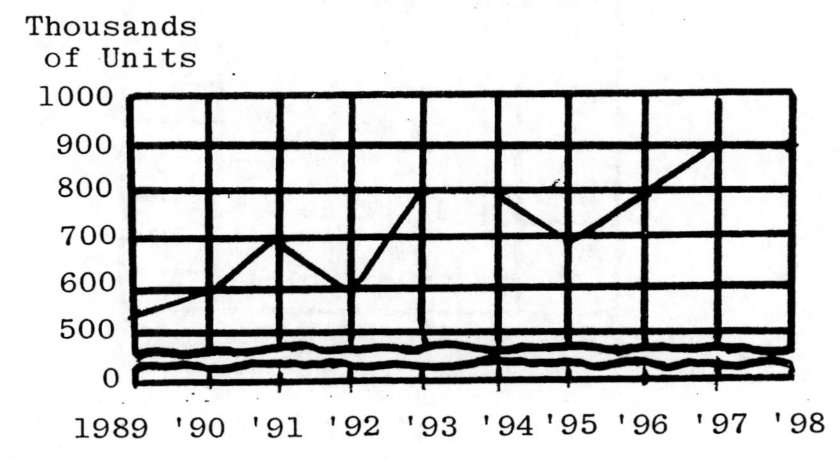

INCREASE IN THE NUMBER OF UNITS OF WORK PRODUCED IN 1998 OVER THE NUMBER PRODUCED IN 1989, BY BOROUGH

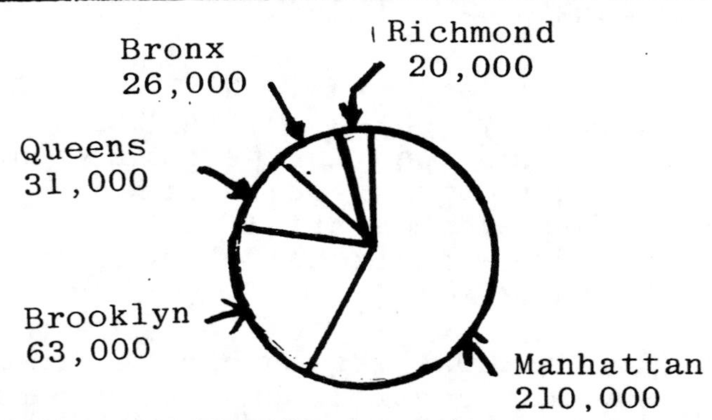

NUMBER OF MALE AND FEMALE EMPLOYEES PRODUCING THE UNITS OF WORK IN THE BUREAU PER YEAR

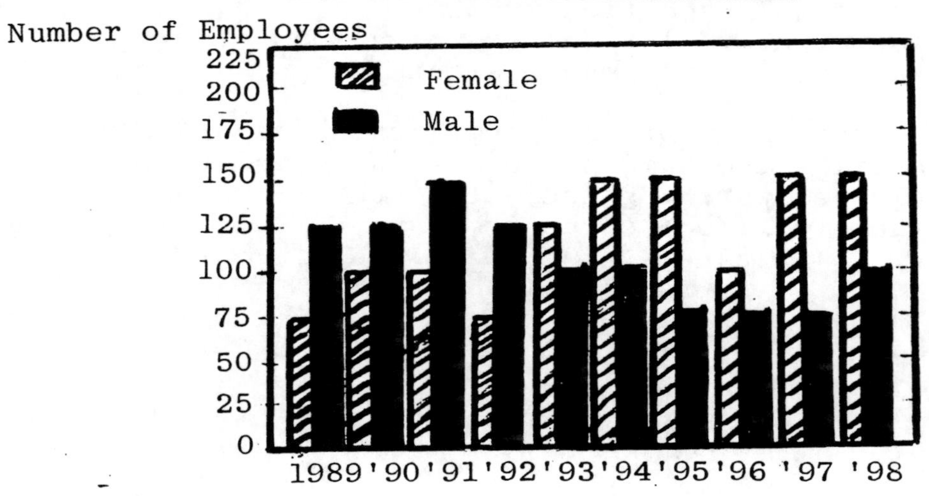

DISTRIBUTION OF THE AGES BY PER CENT, OF EMPLOYEES ASSIGNED TO PRODUCE THE UNITS OF WORK IN THE YEARS 1989 AND 1998

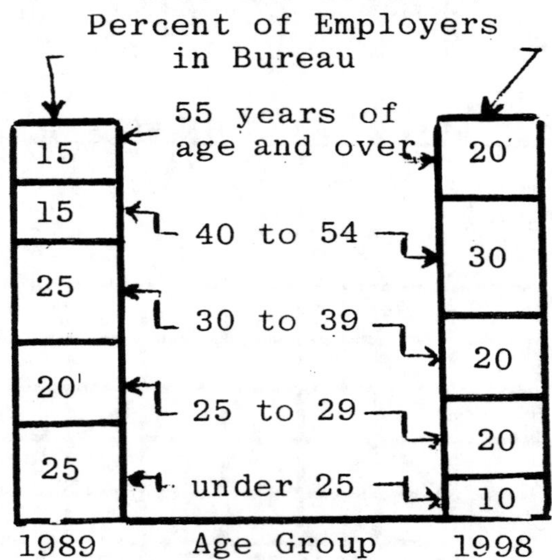

TOTAL SALARIES PAID PER YEAR TO EMPLOYEES ASSIGNED TO PRODUCE THE UNITS OF WORK IN THE BUREAU

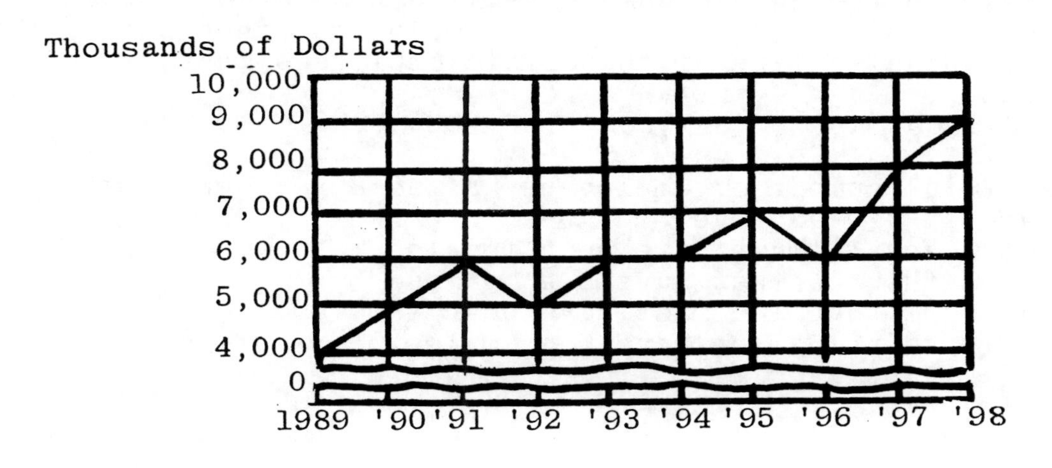

40. The information contained in the charts is sufficient to determine the — 40.____
   A. amount of money paid in salaries to employees working in Richmond in 1998
   B. difference between the average annual salary of employees in the Bureau in 1998 and their average annual salary in 1997
   C. number of female employees in the Bureau between 30 and 39 years of age who were employed in 1989
   D. cost, in salary, for the average male employee in the Bureau to produce 100 units of work in 1994

41. The one of the following which was GREATER in the Bureau in 1994 than it was in 1992 was the — 41.____
   A. cost, in salaries, of producing a unit of work
   B. units of work produced annually per employee
   C. proportion of female employees to total number of employees
   D. average annual salary per employee

42. If, in 1998, one-half of the employees in the Bureau 55 years of age and over each earned an annual salary of $42,000, then the average annual salary of all the remaining employees in the Bureau was MOST NEARLY — 42.____
   A. $31,750 B. $34,500 C. $35,300 D. $35,800

43. Assume that, in 1989, the offices in Richmond and the Bronx each produced the same number of units of work. Also assume that, in 1989, the offices in Brooklyn, Manhattan, and Queens each produced twice as many units of work as were produced in either of the other two boroughs.
Then, the number of units of work produced in Brooklyn in 1998 was MOST NEARLY — 43.____
   A. 69,000 B. 138,000 C. 201,000 D. 225,000

44. If, in 1996, the average annual salary of the female employees in the Bureau was four-fifths as large as the average annual salary of the male employees, then the average annual salary of the female employees in that year was 44.____

A. $37,500 B. $31,000 C. $30,500 D. $30,000

45. Of the total number of employees in the Bureau who were 30 years of age and over in 1989, 45.____

A. at least 35 must have been females
B. less than 75 must have been males
C. no more than 100 must have been females
D. more than 15 must have been males

KEY (CORRECT ANSWERS)

1. D	11. D	21. C	31. B	41. B
2. C	12. C	22. C	32. C	42. C
3. C	13. A	23. A	33. B	43. C
4. D	14. B	24. C	34. A	44. D
5. A	15. A	25. B	35. D	45. A
6. C	16. D	26. D	36. B	
7. A	17. A	27. C	37. C	
8. A	18. A	28. D	38. D	
9. D	19. B	29. A	39. A	
10. B	20. D	30. B	40. B	

EXAMINATION SECTION
TEST 1

DIRECTIONS: Each question or incomplete statement is followed by several suggested answers or completions. Select the one that BEST answers the question or completes the statement. *PRINT THE LETTER OF THE CORRECT ANSWER IN THE SPACE AT THE RIGHT.*

1. In working to establish whether a client is a definite job-counseling case, a counselor's most important clue is 1.___
   A. the counselor's overall evaluation of what the client has said so far, plus an evaluation of nonverbal since the interview started
   B. the feelings, needs, or pressures indicated by the client's words
   C. any comments or recommendations made by a referring professional
   D. the client's statement of her problem

2. Which of the following types of clients would MOST likely be experiencing severe financial problems? 2.___
   A. Culturally different clients
   B. Former military personnel
   C. Displaced homemakers
   D. Voluntary *midlife changers*

3. Which of the following multiple attitude tests is generally considered by job counseling professionals to be the most well-researched? 3.___
   A. Differential Aptitude Test (DAT)
   B. Flanagan Aptitude Classification Test (FACT)
   C. General Aptitude Test Battery (GATB)
   D. Otis-Lennon Mental Ability Test (OLMAT)

4. Approximately what percentage of the job-seeking population knows what they want to do for a living or what jobs match their needs? 4.___
   A. 5-10 B. 20-30 C. 25-40 D. 50-70

5. Which of the following is/are poor choices for an on-the-job tryout? 5.___
   I. An engineering student who is encountering difficulty in choosing among research, applied, sales, and training options
   II. A recent GED recipient who wants to learn about the responsibilities of a paralegal assistant
   III. A high school graduate who wants to learn about the work of a night custodian
   IV. A college graduate with a biology degree who wants to learn about the different types of work in the field of nursing

   The CORRECT answer is:
   A. I, II B. II, IV
   C. I, III, IV D. All of the above

6. Which of the following statements about newspaper want ads is FALSE? 6.____
They
   A. typically represent hiring by last resort
   B. typically account for about 30-40% of the job leads that result in work
   C. tend to be skewed toward low-paying, high-turnover jobs and highly specialized occupations
   D. are usually the first place job seekers should look for jobs

7. Ideally, any *small talk* that is used to make a job-seeking client comfortable during an initial meeting should be 7.____
   A. of mutual interest
   B. centered on the client
   C. neutral
   D. focused on the counselor

8. Which of the following are significant DISADVANTAGES associated with seeking job search or career advice from employers and other experts? 8.____
   I. Such appearances or interviews rarely lead to concrete job leads and may be considered a waste of time by clients or students.
   II. Unhappy or burned-out advisers may discourage qualified and able applicants.
   III. Each expert is a potential source of personal prejudice.

   The CORRECT answer is:
   A. I *only*
   B. I, II
   C. II, III
   D. All of the above

9. Which of the following questions is considered to be unlawful during a job interview? 9.____
   A. Where do you live?
   B. How old are you?
   C. Which languages other than English are you able to read, write or speak?
   D. Have you ever used another name?

10. Which of the following is NOT a guideline for using want ads in a job search? 10.____
   A. *Apply in person* means an applicant may call if he or she does not own car.
   B. Want ads addresses and phone numbers are usually all right to apply for.
   C. Sunday papers are a good source of want ads for the next week.
   D. It may be a good idea to write one's own *job wanted* ad to let employers know they have skills and want work.

11. Typically, it takes about _____ mass-mailed resumes for a job seeker to get one interview offer. 11.____
   A. 10
   B. 70
   C. 120
   D. 250

12. A counselor often works with clients who are described as *disadvantaged* -- a broad term encompassing cultural, educational, environmental, economic, physical, social, and psychological deprivation. Each of the following is typical of the communication pattern of such clients, EXCEPT it is 12.___
   A. temporal rather than spatial
   B. physical and visual rather than auditory
   C. externally oriented, rather than introspective
   D. inductive, rather than deductive

13. Although the Americans With Disabilities Act and most state laws permit employers to use pre-employment medical examinations, they must meet certain requirements. Which of the following is NOT typically one of these? They 13.___
   A. must be applied uniformly to all applicants
   B. must be conducted after an offer of employment is extended
   C. may not include a test for the HIV virus or AIDS
   D. must be job-related

14. Which of the following tests is most appropriate for measuring the readiness of individuals to make choices about vocational issues? 14.___
   A. Differential Aptitude Tests (DAT)
   B. Kuder General Interest Survey
   C. Guilford-Zimmerman Survey
   D. Career Development Inventory (CDI)

15. A career professional wants to allow a client to perform a work tryout, but feels that encountering the negative feelings of others employed in the work setting could be very damaging to the client. The counselor's BEST course would be to involve the client in a _____ program. 15.___
   A. volunteer work experience
   B. cooperative education
   C. simulated work experience
   D. work-study

16. The MOST commonly used type of educational media in vocational counseling is/are 16.___
   A. computer-assisted guidance
   B. programmed instructional materials
   C. printed matter
   D. audio-visual media

17. Which of the following is NOT a significant difference between group career counseling and group career guidance? Group 17.___
   A. guidance is only indirectly concerned with attitudes and behaviors
   B. counseling is intended for clients with temporary problems which require more than mere information

C. guidance procedures can more often be used with large groups
D. counseling is intended to be instructional; group guidance deals with self-discovery

18. The typical job search involves about _____ rejections for each single offer to be interviewed. 18.___
A. 5 B. 15 C. 30 D. 50

19. According to the Employment and Training ADMINISTRATION'S DICTIONARY OF OCCUPATIONAL TITLES (DOT), which of the following is an operative? 19.___
A. Garbage collector B. Machinist
C. Welder D. Carpenter

20. Which of the following should be avoided when preparing a resume? 20.___
A. Focusing on the needs and aspirations of the job seeker
B. Writing short sentences and statements
C. Using examples to illustrate skills or abilities
D. Using type style, headings, and bullets (•) to accentuate certain elements

21. Which of the following is a personality/attitude assessment that is suggested as appropriate for individuals of college age and older? 21.___
A. Otis-Lennon Mental Ability Test (OLMAT)
B. Edwards Personal Preference Schedule (EPPS)
C. Ohio Vocational Interest Survey (OVIS, OVIS II)
D. Work Values Inventory (WVI)

22. Essentially, there are three major purposes for an initial job seeker/counselor interview. Which of the following is NOT one of these? 22.___
A. Agreeing on the structure and plan for further counseling and related activities
B. Establishing a relationship so that counseling can continue
C. Suggesting possible areas of career exploration
D. Establishing the client's needs and feelings

23. Which of the following is a functional job skill? 23.___
A. Tolerating stress B. Persistence
C. Imagination D. Writing

24. When a client or student names and describes a *dream job*, each of the following is an important response in the early stages of a job search EXCEPT 24.___
A. linking his/her aspirations with immediate, practical steps toward the long-term goal
B. reinforcing or validating the dream choice
C. finding out why he/she chose it
D. cautioning him/her if the job seems outrageous or impractical

25. Educational media in vocational counseling tend to be LEAST effective when 25.___
   A. they are introduced carefully and conspicuously into the program
   B. they are applied to small, isolated educational problems
   C. the media developer and the counselor select materials together
   D. they are integrated into the entire program

KEY (CORRECT ANSWERS)

1. A
2. C
3. C
4. B
5. B

6. D
7. A
8. C
9. B
10. A

11. D
12. A
13. C
14. D
15. C

16. C
17. D
18. B
19. C
20. A

21. B
22. C
23. D
24. D
25. B

TEST 2

DIRECTIONS: Each question or incomplete statement is followed by several suggested answers or completions. Select the one that BEST answers the question or completes the statement. *PRINT THE LETTER OF THE CORRECT ANSWER IN THE SPACE AT THE RIGHT.*

1. Which of the following statements about interviewing for a job is TRUE? 1.____
   A. A screening interviewer is looking for a reason to accept a candidate, rather than a reason to reject him.
   B. In a nondirective interview, a candidate is permitted to talk about anything he likes.
   C. A candidate should volunteer nothing in a screening interview.
   D. Interviewers will never intentionally introduce stress into an interview situation.

2. Each of the following are disadvantages associated with a holistic life-career planning process EXCEPT 2.____
   A. it does not address the important issue of a job seeker's marketable skills
   B. it can overemphasize the nature of individual decision-making
   C. it tends to equate one's worth and life with his work
   D. the possibility of making a poor choice is much more frightening to first-time job seekers

3. When an employer begins to hire and is considering potential employees, she is typically LEAST concerned with 3.____
   A. the number of years or months of work experience that is directly related to the position
   B. whether a candidate will be easy to train
   C. whether a candidate will stay on the job after being trained
   D. the quality of a candidate's work habits

4. It is generally agreed that job counselors use standardized tests for a few specific purposes. Which of the following is NOT one of these? 4.____
   A. Diagnosis B. Prediction
   C. Placement D. Monitoring

5. In general, 70-90% of employees who are fired from their jobs are let go because 5.____
   A. their job skills are poorly matched to the position
   B. they have inappropriate social skills or poor work habits
   C. they have committed one or more serious and costly errors
   D. they cannot handle the workload

6. According to the Employment and Training ADMINISTRATION'S DICTIONARY OF OCCUPATIONAL TITLES (DOT), which of the following is a benchwork occupation? 6.___
   A. Bank teller
   B. Sheet-metal worker
   C. Piano tuner
   D. Punch press operator

7. Once a job seeker has been taught phone skills, he or she should call each employer _____ before considering the job lead *dead*. 7.___
   A. once
   B. twice
   C. three times
   D. five times

8. In general, which of the following can be defined as the ultimate outcomes or goals of job search training? 8.___
   I. Learning how to find employers by networking and persistence
   II. Selecting a life-long career in the field of one's primary interest
   III. Learning how to describe one's interests and marketable skills in a positive and detailed manner

   The CORRECT answer is:
   A. I *only*
   B. II *only*
   C. I, III
   D. All of the above

9. Each of the following is a way in which work experience programs can increase the motivation for learning in disadvantaged clients EXCEPT 9.___
   A. developing specific occupational skills
   B. increasing feelings of self-worth
   C. leading to specific job leads
   D. helping clients find the financial assistance needed to remain in school

10. Which of the following is a disadvantage associated with the use of the Flanagan Aptitude Classification Test (FACT) for determining a client's vocational skills? 10.___
    A. Test accessories tend to be badly organized and sketchy.
    B. Tests are usually not considered to be interesting or challenging.
    C. The basic assumption of measuring identified job elements and combining test of those basic elements to estimate possible success does not always appear logical.
    D. It is of limited value for clients who are considering occupations that require college preparation.

11. The ideal time for a job seeker to give her resume to a potential employer is 11.___
    A. on the first contact, with an explanatory letter
    B. after making an appointment for a personal interview
    C. right at the beginning of a personal interview
    D. after a personal interview

12. Which of the following behaviors is most likely to make an applicant appear overly familiar during an interview? 12.___
   A. Raised eyebrows
   B. Shuffling feet
   C. Shrugging
   D. Leaning back

13. Which of the following is an adaptive job skill? 13.___
   A. Planning
   B. Analyzing
   C. Being courteous
   D. Memorizing

14. A rule of thumb for resume preparation is that about _____% of the page should remain blank or empty. 14.___
   A. 5
   B. 10
   C. 30
   D. 50

15. Each of the following is an important difference between technical and nontechnical skills in the job market EXCEPT 15.___
   A. technical skills set the basic requirements for a job
   B. all jobs require a variety of nontechnical skills
   C. nontechnical skills determine success beyond a basic level
   D. all jobs have readily identifiable technical skills

16. The main problem with using printed and audio-visual materials as educational media in job counseling is that they 16.___
   A. may move the client too quickly through the job-choice process
   B. retain their usability longer than their accuracy
   C. tend to restrict the role of the counselor
   D. may present too much information to a client at once

17. Which of the following career/job search materials or resources is most likely to be used at the latest phase in the selection process? 17.___
   A. Work tryout experience
   B. Printed guidance materials
   C. Interviews with trainers
   D. Computerized materials

18. While many clients have difficulty finding a job right away, some clients fail to find a job at all. Each of the following is usually involved in such a situation EXCEPT 18.___
   A. the client is not sure about how to begin an effective job search
   B. there are few to no jobs in the client's particular field of interest or expertise
   C. the client gives up looking for work too soon
   D. the client feels that there are many weak points in his/her past

19. When working with a job seeker who is an ex-offender or drug addict, the BEST course of action is probably to 19.___
   A. connect the client to a parole officer or drug counselor who can locate an ex-offender or recovered person who might be interviewed first
   B. contact an advocate from a local office who will strenuously promote the client's job applications

C. instruct the client to avoid mentioning this aspect of his/her history to potential employers, unless asked about it directly
D. limit job applications to jobs that involve structured, unskilled tasks

20. During a job interview, an interviewer sometimes appears to be imposing periods of silence. Usually, this is because the interviewer 20.___
A. is testing the candidate to see how he reacts to imposed stress
B. is manifesting her own confidence in the situation
C. would like the candidate to elaborate on a response
D. lacks experience and is formulating the next question

21. When using interest inventories in client exploration, counselors should typically be aware of common problems associated with their application. Which of the following is NOT one of these problems? 21.___
A. Scores may produce a very abbreviated list of suggested occupations.
B. There are few reliable interest inventories that are keyed directly to occupational options.
C. The objective information produced by the scores often leads to insufficient counseling.
D. Clients are often inclined to focus attention on interest scores to confirm their own subjective evaluations, and then move their attention to occupations suggested by those scores.

22. Large group instruction is sometimes used in job search or career education, but it has the significant DISADVANTAGE of 22.___
A. requiring credentialed educators
B. disseminating large amounts of information to numerous individuals at once
C. absorbing too much of the client's job search responsibilities
D. not allowing for group interaction or individual clarification of information

23. A newspaper want ad states that an applicant for a position must have 3-5 years experience in the field. Typically, a client should be encouraged to apply if he has 23.___
A. no experience in the field but is willing to learn
B. less than one year of experience
C. one year of experience plus other skills
D. more than 10 years experience in the field

24. The Strong-Campbell Interest Inventory (SCII) is generally considered to be a useful career-planning tool for each of the following types of job-seekers EXCEPT those who 24.___

A. are able to identify some of their likes and dislikes
B. appear to have some understanding of their career potentials
C. are considering occupations involving college preparation
D. appear to be personally confused about the direction their lives are taking

25. Which of the following is NOT an advantage associated with the use of programmed or mechanized materials (workbooks or sequenced exercises) as educational media in job counseling? 25.___
They
A. allow the client to proceed at a personally determined pace
B. increase feelings of personalization with each client
C. assist the client in obtaining information and to process that information in a way that logically moves her toward a decision
D. assure that specific steps are mastered before advancing to later steps

---

KEY (CORRECT ANSWERS)

1. C
2. A
3. A
4. C
5. B

6. C
7. C
8. C
9. C
10. D

11. D
12. D
13. C
14. C
15. D

16. B
17. A
18. B
19. A
20. A

21. B
22. D
23. C
24. D
25. B

EXAMINATION SECTION

TEST 1

DIRECTIONS: Each question or incomplete statement is followed by several suggested answers or completions. Select the one that BEST answers the question or completes the statement. *PRINT THE LETTER OF THE CORRECT ANSWER IN THE SPACE AT THE RIGHT.*

1. The MOST reliable federal source for information about labor conditions is the monthly reports issued by the Department of 1.___
   A. Commerce B. Defense C. Interior D. Labor

2. In a labor-management dispute that threatens the national health and safety, the President of the United States may, under the provisions of the Labor-Management Relations Act, 2.___
   A. take over the struck plant until a settlement is reached
   B. request an injunction prohibiting a strike for 80 days
   C. require the parties to the dispute to submit their differences to arbitration
   D. appoint the Secretary of Labor to mediate the dispute

3. The majority of workers in the United States belong to 3.___
   A. the AFL-CIO B. a national union
   C. independent unions D. none of the above

4. The Economic Opportunity Act of 1964 does NOT provide for 4.___
   A. education programs
   B. loans to low-income farmers and businessmen
   C. minimum wage rates for workers
   D. work programs

5. Which of the following statements is TRUE? 5.___
   A. The Equal Pay Act of 1963 amends the Fair Labor Standards Act by prohibiting wage discrimination on the basis of sex.
   B. The Equal Pay Act prohibits under all circumstances payment at lower rates to one sex than to the other.
   C. An employer may reduce the rate of a male employee to make it equal to the rate of a female employee and thus comply with the provisions of the Equal Pay Act of 1963.
   D. An employer and a union may waive the provisions of the Equal Pay Act of 1963 so as to allow wage differentials based on sex.

6. The whole or partial closing of a business establishment in order to gain concessions from employees is termed a 6.___
   A. strike B. lockout
   C. work stoppage D. slowdown

7. The civilian labor force in the United States (both employed and unemployed) in the mid-1990's is APPROXIMATELY _____ million. 7.___
   A. 100 B. 115 C. 130 D. 150

8. The number of states having a *right to work* law is MOST NEARLY 8.___
   A. 10 B. 20 C. 30 D. 40

9. The term *business unionism* is used to describe the kind of union whose PRINCIPAL purpose is to 9.___
   A. advance the immediate interests of its members
   B. make its leaders well off at the expense of the members
   C. make the businessmen with whom it bargains as properous as possible
   D. preserve the strength of the industry

10. The FIRST national organization of workers to be formed in the United States and still in existence is the 10.___
    A. International Ladies' Garment Workers Union
    B. Typographical Union
    C. United Mine Workers
    D. United Textile Workers

11. The Fair Employment Practices Law permits employment agencies, when interviewing job applicants, to ask for information concerning the applicant's 11.___
    A. nationality B. previous experience
    C. religion D. parents' birthplace

12. A MAJOR concession sought by striking professional athletes has been 12.___
    A. a shorter season
    B. free agency
    C. unemployment compensation
    D. guaranteed contracts

13. In order to be eligible for unemployment compensation in the State of New York, a jobless claimant MUST 13.___
    A. have been laid off for other than disciplinary reasons
    B. be ready, willing, and able to work at any job or rate of pay comparable with his previous employment
    C. be available in New York for work that is offered
    D. refuse to participate in a strike

14. A worker was injured on the job and won an award of 50% permanent partial disability from the Workmen's Compensation Board. He reported back to work but the employer refused to put him back on the basis that he couldn't be expected to handle the work. The union refused to take his case to arbitration on the ground that the employer was within his rights.
You should tell him
   A. that the union's action was proper
   B. to complain to the National Labor Relations Board
   C. to refer the matter to the Bureau of Labor-Management Reports
   D. to complain to the Workmen's Compensation Board

14.___

15. One of the workers in a novelty manufacturing plant with 200 employees complains that the union in his shop refused to handle his grievance because he is not a member of the union. The plant is covered by a union contract which does not require all employees covered by the contract to become members of the union.
You should tell him
   A. to complain to the National Labor Relations Board
   B. to complain to the State Department of Labor
   C. to complain to the Bureau of Labor-Management Reports
   D. that he has no valid complaint

15.___

16. A worker complains that, after his union won a National Labor Relations Board election in his shop, the union negotiated and signed a contract with the employer without a ratification vote by the members of the shop.
You should tell him
   A. to refer it to the National Labor Relations Board
   B. to refer the matter to the State Labor Board
   C. to contact the Bureau of Labor-Management Reports
   D. that he has no valid complaint

16.___

17. A worker complains that his employer fired him that morning but told him to come back on Friday, the usual payday, for his pay. The union was unable to get the employer to change his position.
You should tell the discharged worker
   A. to complain to the Small Claims Court
   B. to refer the matter to the National Labor Relations Board
   C. that he has no valid complaint
   D. to contact the District Attorney

17.___

18. A worker complains that he was laid off the day after he had an argument with the business agent when the business agent refused to give him a copy of the union agreement. A new worker was hired on his job the same day he was laid off. The union refused to handle his grievance.
You should tell him
   A. to refer it to the National Labor Relations Board

18.___

B. to report it to the Bureau of Labor-Management Reports
C. to contact the State Labor Department
D. that the union's action was proper

19. The client, a man who works in a button factory, complains that he was denied promotion because of his race. He indicates a belief that his foreman, Mr. Joseph Smith, may possibly have been responsible. The story sounds confused, and the interviewer asks a clarifying question. Which of the following is an example of poor questioning? 19.___
A. Do you think that Joe was the guy who kept you from getting the promotion?
B. Was Mr. Smith the man who you think blocked your promotion?
C. Don't you think it was the foreman who was trying to keep you down?
D. Do you get along well with Mr. Smith?

20. A worker brings you a petition signed by 150 of the 200 workers in his shop that they want to get rid of their union. 20.___
Tell him to
A. go to the State Labor Board
B. contact the National Labor Relations Board
C. go to the Bureau of Labor-Management Reports
D. wait until after the contract has expired before taking any action

21. A union member who is being expelled from the union because of opposition to its policies is NOT entitled to 21.___
A. a set of specific written charges by the union
B. reasonable time to prepare his defense
C. a hearing
D. fees for his attorney

Questions 22-23.

DIRECTIONS: Questions 22 and 23 are to be answered on the basis of the following information.

A contract provides: *In determining an employee's right to a vacation and the length of his vacation his seniority as of June 1st of that calendar year shall govern* and *all employees with one year of seniority shall be entitled to one week of vacation with five days' straight time pay; employees with six years or more of seniority shall be entitled to two weeks of vacation with ten days' straight time pay. Vacations shall be scheduled between June 1st and September 30th of each year.* The company announced that the plant would shut down from July 1st to July 15, during which time all workers entitled to vacations would be required to take their vacations.

22. Worker Jones started to work for the company June 15. He complains that the company refused to give him any vacation pay and that the union refused to process his grievance for one week's vacation pay.
You should tell him
A. to appeal to the union's executive board
B. to complain to the National Labor Relations Board
C. to complain to the Bureau of Labor Management Reports
D. that he has no valid claim

22.___

23. Worker Smith started work for the company on May 30th. He complains that he received only five days' straight time pay although he was entitled to receive seven days' vacation pay and that the union refused to take up his grievance.
You should tell him
A. to complain to the National Labor Relations Board
B. to complain to the Bureau of Labor Management Reports
C. to complain to the District Attorney
D. that he has no valid claim

23.___

24. The percentage of union members in the labor force since 1980 has
A. decreased
B. increased
C. remained stable
D. fluctuated

24.___

25. An illegal labor strike in which the striking members defied a back-to-work order and were dismissed by President Reagan involved
A. baseball players
B. air traffic controllers
C. farm workers
D. mine workers

25.___

KEY (CORRECT ANSWERS)

1. D
2. B
3. D
4. C
5. A

6. B
7. C
8. B
9. A
10. B

11. B
12. B
13. B
14. A
15. A

16. D
17. C
18. A
19. C
20. B

21. D
22. D
23. D
24. A
25. B

TEST 2

DIRECTIONS: Each question or incomplete statement is followed by several suggested answers or completions. Select the one that BEST answers the question or completes the statement. *PRINT THE LETTER OF THE CORRECT ANSWER IN THE SPACE AT THE RIGHT.*

1. Below is a list of labor unions operating in New York City. Which of the designations is INCORRECT? 1.___
   A. Blueprint, Photostat & Photo Employees - International Jewelry Workers Union, AFL-CIO
   B. Pizzeria, Hero & Dining Room Employees - Amalgamated Union
   C. Private Sanitation Union - International Brotherhood of Teamsters, Chauffeurs, Warehousemen & Helpers
   D. Department Store Employees Union - Retail, Wholesale & Department Store Union, AFL-CIO

2. Which of the following is an example of a secondary boycott? 2.___
   An
   A. appeal by a union to the public not to buy the goods of an employer with whom it has a dispute
   B. appeal by a union to members of another union not to buy the goods of an employer with whom the first union has a dispute
   C. attempt by a striking union to prevent workers from taking the jobs of those workers who are on strike
   D. attempt to exert pressure against a *neutral* employer in order to persuade him to exert pressure against the employer with whom a union has a dispute

3. Which of the following is an example of an escalator clause in a labor agreement? 3.___
   A. Straight time hourly rates shall be increased by 2% each year during the life of the agreement.
   B. Straight time hourly rates shall be changed by 1% each quarter for every 2 percentage points' change in the consumer price index.
   C. Meritorious employees shall be eligible for increase of 2% in straight time hourly pay once a year upon the recommendation of the Personnel Division.
   D. The number of hours in the work week shall be decreased by one hour each year, with a 5 cent increase in the base rate of pay.

4. The United States Government is devoted to the principle of equal employment opportunities for all its citizens. Proper employee selection by employers is essential. Government emphasis has been directed toward insuring that this selection is done on a basis of 4.___

A. additional training for underprivileged individuals, regardless of sex, race or religion
B. objective merit rather than prejudice
C. potential for development rather than ability to perform
D. quotas for all minority groups

5. The Bureau of the Census officially defines the labor force as those persons who, at the time a census survey is made, have a job or are looking for work and are age ____ and over. 5.___
A. 14 B. 16 C. 18 D. 21

6. The Taft-Hartley Act is also known as the ____ Act. 6.___
A. Economic Opportunity
B. Fair Labor Standards
C. Labor-Management Relations
D. National Labor Relations

7. Under the federal Labor-Management Relations Act, as amended, which of the following is NOT an unfair labor practice for a labor union? 7.___
A. Coercing a worker into joining a union in an unorganized shop
B. Fining a member for refusing to attend union meetings
C. Forcing an employer to discharge a member who has openly criticized the local president
D. Requiring an employer to hire only workers who are union members in good standing

8. The Manpower Development and Training Act (MDTA) authorizes expanded vocational training on the job and in school. Which of the following statements is INCONSISTENT with the Act? 8.___
A. Unemployed workers can upgrade their skills under MDTA programs.
B. The proximity of training to the work environment is the key feature of on-the-job training.
C. Trainees are eligible to receive training allowances under certain conditions.
D. Employers are ineligible for any reimbursement for training costs.

9. The federal government considers a locality a distressed area when the percentage of the labor force unemployed is AT LEAST 9.___
A. 4% B. 6% C. 8% D. 10%

10. The federal statute requiring the government to *deal with the problem of unemployment resulting from automation and technological changes and other types of persistent unemployment* is the ____ Act. 10.___
A. Civil Rights
B. Economic Opportunity
C. Fair Labor Standards
D. Manpower Development and Training

11. A *sweetheart agreement* may be defined as an agreement 11.___
    A. entered into by the union and the employer without the knowledge of the employees
    B. entered into between the employer and employees without the knowledge of the union
    C. between the union and the employees covering members' rights
    D. among employers in the same industry to maintain uniform conditions

12. Which of the following definitions is USUALLY applied to the phrase *managerial prerogatives*? 12.___
    The rights of
    A. the proprietor which have remained with him, despite a union contract
    B. supervisors to receive more privileges than union members
    C. the Board of Directors in relation to the stockholders
    D. the state to supervise business enterprises

13. Which of the following is in compliance with a provision of the law in New York State? 13.___
    A. The employer may not make deductions from wages for damage to equipment or materials.
    B. Children under 16 years of age can get permits to do industrial homework.
    C. Private employment agencies are not governed by state law.
    D. The State Labor Department operates apprenticeship training programs.

14. Which of the organizations below serves as collective bargaining representative for some of its members? 14.___
    American _____ Association.
    A. Medical B. Nurses'
    C. Bar D. Arbitration

15. A company open 5 days a week and employing 28 office workers allows its office workers a 15 minute coffee break every day. 15.___
    Assuming that the average pay of these workers is $9.20 per hour, what is the weekly cost of these coffee breaks?
    A. $317.00 B. $320.00 C. $322.00 D. $351.00

16. Employees who are entitled to the minimum wage under the federal Fair Labor Standards Act and who have received less than this CANNOT collect from their employer the amount owed to them by 16.___
    A. suing the employer themselves
    B. asking the United States Secretary of Labor to sue the employer in their behalf
    C. filing a complaint with the United States Bureau of Labor Standards
    D. filing a complaint with the Wage and Hour and Public Contracts Division

17. Under federal and state laws, which of the following collective bargaining agreement provisions is UNLAWFUL? 17.___
   A. All persons in the bargaining unit who have worked in the shop for more than 60 days must join the union in order to keep their jobs.
   B. Any worker who arrives late more than three times in a row may be discharged without a hearing.
   C. The employer shall pay the sum of 5¢ per hour per employee into a jointly managed welfare fund for the benefit of union members only.
   D. An employee who has been expelled from the union for refusal to pay union dues shall be discharged.

18. Mrs. Rivera is employed as a machine operator at the Triangle Shirt Company. She works 5 days a week from 9 A.M. to 5 P.M. with one hour for lunch. She earns $7.80 per hour and time and a half for overtime. If, in addition to the regular work week, she worked last week three evenings until 7:30 P.M., her weekly earnings amounted to 18.___
   A. $312.00   B. $399.75   C. $405.25   D. $468.00

19. A worker over 65 years of age retired this year after working 30 years in union shops in the same industry, ten years under each of three different locals in the AFL-CIO. Each local union contract provided for retirement with pension at or after age 65 for employees with at least 15 years of credited service, and each provided for 1 year of credited service for each year of employment under the contract, and for payment of $2.00 per month for each year of credited service. 19.___
The worker is _____ pension.
   A. entitled to $60 per month
   B. entitled to $30 per month
   C. entitled to $20 per month
   D. not entitled to any

20. The average family income in the United States in the mid-1990's was estimated to be APPROXIMATELY 20.___
   A. $15,000   B. $19,000   C. $23,000   D. $28,000

21. The name of the reporter who covered the Triangle Shirtwaist Co. fire in New York and later became Secretary of Labor is 21.___
   A. Goldberg   B. Mitchell   C. Perkins   D. Wirtz

22. The *patterned interview* is a device used by sophisticated employers to 22.___
   A. select employees who fit the ethnic pattern of the community
   B. ascertain the pattern of facts surrounding a grievance
   C. discourage workers from joining unions
   D. appraise a subject's most important character traits

23. Which of the following is an example of a *non-directive* interview? 23.___
The
    A. subject directs his remarks at someone other than the interviewer
    B. subject discusses any topics that seem to be relevant to him
    C. subject has not been directed that he need answer any particular question
    D. interview is confined to the facts of the case, and is not directed at eliciting personal information

24. When interviewing a person, the interviewer may easily slip into error in rating his subject's personal qualities because of the general impression he receives of the individual. 24.___
This tendency is known as the
    A. *halo* effect
    B. subjective bias problem
    C. *person-to-person* error
    D. inflation effect

25. An interviewer would find an interview checklist LEAST useful for 25.___
    A. making sure that all the principal facts are secured in the interview
    B. insuring that the claimant's grievance is settled in his favor
    C. facilitating later research into the nature of the problems handled by the agency
    D. conducting the interview in a logical and orderly fashion

---

KEY (CORRECT ANSWERS)

1. D
2. D
3. B
4. B
5. B
6. C
7. B
8. D
9. D
10. D
11. A
12. A
13. A
14. B
15. C
16. C
17. C
18. B
19. D
20. C
21. C
22. D
23. B
24. A
25. B

EXAMINATION SECTION
TEST 1

DIRECTIONS: Each question or incomplete statement is followed by several suggested answers or completions. Select the one that BEST answers the question or completes the statement. *PRINT THE LETTER OF THE CORRECT ANSWER IN THE SPACE AT THE RIGHT.*

1. The process in which a neutral makes a binding decision in a dispute between two parties is known as 1.___
   A. mediation B. arbitration
   C. conciliation D. fact-finding

2. Mediation is PRIMARILY a process for 2.___
   A. getting disputing parties to talk to each other in a civil manner
   B. listening to both sides patiently
   C. persuading both sides to settle their differences sensibly
   D. separating both sides peacefully

3. A check-off provision in a collective bargaining agreement is one by which the employer agrees to deduct 3.___
   A. federal income tax from an employee's gross pay and transmit it directly to the Internal Revenue Service
   B. unemployment insurance tax from an employee's gross pay and transmit it to the Unemployment Insurance Fund
   C. pension and welfare contributions from an employee's gross pay and transmit them to the pension and welfare funds
   D. union dues from an employee's pay and transmit it to the union

4. The term *bargaining unit* refers to a(n) 4.___
   A. group of workers in whose behalf a union bargains
   B. group of workers who belong to the union in a plant
   C. local union that bargains with the employer in a particular plant
   D. international union engaged in multi-employer bargaining

5. A certified union is a 5.___
   A. bona fide union that belongs to the AFL-CIO
   B. union that has not been found guilty of violating the National Labor Relations Act
   C. union whose practices conform to the requirements of the Labor-Management Reporting and Disclosure Act
   D. union that has been designed for bargaining purposes by the National Labor Relations Board or an equivalent state agency

6. One PRINCIPAL difference between a business agent and a shop steward is that a business 6.___
   A. agent is an official appointed by the union whereas a shop steward is always an elected official
   B. agent, unlike a shop steward, is empowered to adjust grievances
   C. agent is employed by the union, whereas a shop steward is an employee of the company
   D. agent pays dues to the union, whereas a shop steward usually does not

7. An international union is BEST described as a labor union that is 7.___
   A. affiliated with the International Conference of Free Trade Unions
   B. affiliated with the International Labor Organization
   C. an American national union with locals in Canada
   D. affiliated with the AFL-CIO

8. The Central Labor Council is an organization 8.___
   A. consisting of all unions in New York City
   B. consisting of all unions in New York City and some of its suburbs
   C. that requires its officers to take a non-Communist oath
   D. affiliated with the AFL-CIO

9. A union that refuses to let its members see a copy of the collective bargaining agreement is violating the _____ Act. 9.___
   A. Labor-Management Reporting and Disclosure
   B. Labor Management Relations
   C. Smoot-Hawley
   D. Pendleton

10. Some collective bargaining agreements provide that when a man is laid off, he may claim the job of another worker who has worked in the shop for a shorter period of time. This practice is referred to as 10.___
    A. sliding B. bumping
    C. pulling rank D. pyramiding

11. Which of the following is a government office? 11.___
    A. Chamber of Commerce B. Community Chest
    C. Department of Labor D. American Red Cross

12. A continuous increase in prices sustained by wage and cost increases reacting to each other is termed a(n) 12.___
    A. inflationary spiral B. cost of living gap
    C. recession D. consumer price index

13. The national minimum wage was FIRST enacted in 13.___
    A. 1924 B. 1938 C. 1944 D. 1957

14. Assume that an individual who had just lost his job asks you where to look for another job. 14.___
Of the following answers, the one that would be LEAST useful to him is:
   A. Read the employer ads in the newspapers
   B. Go to the State Employment Service
   C. Ask your union to help you
   D. Leave your telephone number with your last employer

Questions 15-18.

DIRECTIONS: For each question numbered 15 through 18, select the option whose meaning is MOST NEARLY the same as that of the italicized word.

15. *voluntary* 15.___
   A. by free choice
   B. necessary
   C. important
   D. by design

16. *injunction* 16.___
   A. act of prohibiting
   B. process of inserting
   C. means of arbitrating
   D. freedom of action

17. *amicable* 17.___
   A. compelled
   B. friendly
   C. unimportant
   D. insignificant

18. *closed shop* 18.___
   A. one that employs only members of a union
   B. one that employs union members and unaffiliated employees
   C. one that employs only employees with previous experience
   D. one that employs skilled and unskilled workers

19. A worker complains to you that he was fired from his job without a week's notice. There is no union in his shop. 19.___
You should tell him
   A. to refer it to the National Labor Relations Board
   B. to contact the Wage and Hour and Public Contracts Division
   C. to report it to the Bureau of Labor-Management Reports
   D. that he has no valid complaint

20. A worker complains that he kept asking his union's business agent for a copy of the contract; he even wrote him a registered letter asking for it. He was never given a copy. 20.___
You should tell him
   A. to report it to the Bureau of Labor-Management Reports
   B. to refer it to the National Labor Relations Board
   C. to report it to the New York State Department of Labor
   D. that he has no basis for a complaint

21. A worker complained that he was fired because the employer wanted to make a vacancy for a friend of the foreman. The union took his grievance all the way through arbitration, and the arbitrator ruled against the union. The worker wants to know where he should go to appeal. You should tell him 21.___
   A. to report it to the Bureau of Labor-Management Reports
   B. to refer it to the National Labor Relations Board
   C. to report it to the American Arbitration Association
   D. that he has no basis for an appeal

22. In the collective bargaining process with professional athletes, player representatives assume the role of 22.___
   A. middle management
   B. union delegates
   C. scabs
   D. arbitrators

23. Of the following, the one which is NOT a labor union is the 23.___
   A. Actor's Equity Association
   B. ILGWU
   C. AFT
   D. NAFTA

24. In interviewing a man who has a grievance, it is IMPORTANT that the interviewer 24.___
   A. take note of such physical responses as shifty eyes
   B. use a lie detector, if possible, to ascertain the truth in doubtful situations
   C. allow the complainant to *tell his story*
   D. place the complainant under oath

25. Ideally, the setting for an interview should NOT include 25.___
   A. an informal opening
   B. privacy and comfort
   C. an atmosphere of leisure
   D. a lie detector

KEY (CORRECT ANSWERS)

1. B
2. C
3. D
4. A
5. D

6. C
7. C
8. D
9. A
10. B

11. C
12. A
13. B
14. D
15. A

16. A
17. B
18. A
19. D
20. A

21. D
22. B
23. D
24. C
25. D

TEST 2

DIRECTIONS: Each question or incomplete statement is followed by several suggested answers or completions. Select the one that BEST answers the question or completes the statement. *PRINT THE LETTER OF THE CORRECT ANSWER IN THE SPACE AT THE RIGHT.*

1. Writing up the interview into a systematic report is BEST done 1.___
   A. in the presence of the subject so that mistakes can be corrected immediately
   B. within a reasonably short time after the interview so that nothing is forgotten
   C. no sooner than several days after the interview so that the interviewer will have had plenty of time to think about it
   D. with the help of someone not present at the interview so that an objective view can be obtained

2. When dealing with an aggrieved worker, a USEFUL interviewing technique is to 2.___
   A. maintain a sympathetic attitude
   B. maintain an attitude of cold impartiality
   C. assure the subject that you are on his side
   D. display a tape recorder to give the subject confidence that no parts of his story will be overlooked

3. Special mediators are used MAINLY when 3.___
   A. regular mediators are away on vacation
   B. individuals with specialized background are required to mediate certain labor disputes
   C. there is a backlog of work
   D. there is a change in administration

4. Which of the following is an example of a contributory pension plan? 4.___
   ______ to the Pension Fund.
   A. The employer makes all the contributions
   B. The employees make all the contributions
   C. Employer and employee jointly contribute
   D. Social Security payments are counted as contributions

5. The following provision is found in a collective bargaining agreement: *An employee who reports to work, and who has not been given 24 hours notice that his services are not required that day, shall receive a minimum of four hours' pay.* 5.___
   This provision refers to
   A. the minimum rate
   B. the minimum wage
   C. the penalty rate
   D. call-in pay

6. Workers sometimes make an informal agreement among themselves to limit output in the shop. When a worker works just hard enough to reach his share of the limit, he is said to be 6.___
   A. making the *bogey*   B. swinging the cat
   C. seeing the man   D. horsing around

7. Under the Fair Employment Practices Law, which of the following questions may an employer ask a prospective employee? 7.___
   A. What nationality are you?
   B. Where were your parents born?
   C. What church do you attend?
   D. From what school did you graduate?

8. An employer has refused to accepted telephoned suggestions from you for settling a complaint regarding alleged unfair treatment in his plant. Which of the following methods would you NOT use to influence him? 8.___
   A. Write him a letter.
   B. Assign a staff member to visit him to explain the procedures of the department.
   C. Request inspectors from several city departments to inspect his plant to uncover violations.
   D. Call him in for a conference.

9. A factory employee who is injured in the course of his employment generally has the right to 9.___
   A. use an attorney to press his claim
   B. sue his employer in the courts of the state, although the employer carries Workmen's Compensation insurance
   C. sue his employer in federal court if he is engaged in interstate commerce, although the employer carries Workmen's Compensation insurance
   D. go to the American Arbitration Association to press his claim

10. Of the following occupation groups in the United States, the one that has the GREATEST number of female workers is the _____ group. 10.___
   A. clerical and kindred workers
   B. professional, technical, and kindred workers
   C. sales workers
   D. service workers

11. The National Labor Relations Act, also known as the Wagner Act, 11.___
   A. specifies the minimum wage for employees engaged in interstate commerce
   B. guarantees to employees the right to organize without employer interference
   C. forbids the employment of children in industries engaged in interstate commerce
   D. stipulates that employers pay time and a half to employees after forty hours of work in any week

12. Which of the following statutes is known as the Anti-Injunction Act? 12.___
The _____ Act.
   A. Walsh-Healey
   B. Wagner-Peyser
   C. Davis-Bacon
   D. Norris-LaGuardia

13. A worker complains that his employer is making payroll deductions for social security, income tax, and United States savings bonds without his consent. 13.___
You should tell him that the
   A. employer has a patriotic duty to deduct for United States savings bonds from all of his employees
   B. employee must authorize a deduction for United States savings bonds
   C. employer requires authorization from the employee to deduct for social security and income tax
   D. employer is in his right and that he has no valid complaint

14. A group of workers complain that they were not paid for Thanksgiving Day. They show you their union contract which provides for Thanksgiving Day as a holiday with pay for each employee unless the employee doesn't work the day before or the day after the holiday. They all worked on the Wednesday before Thanksgiving but, because the employer shut the whole shop down on the Friday after Thanksgiving, they did not work again until the following Monday. 14.___
What should they do?
   A. Complain to the National Labor Relations Board.
   B. File a grievance with the union.
   C. Complain to the Bureau of Labor-Management Reports.
   D. Complain to the Mediation Board.

15. A worker makes the following complaint: *I was laid off without pay on Thanksgiving Day. I worked on the following Saturday but was not paid time and a half for the Saturday work. There is no union in my plant.* 15.___
You should tell him
   A. to report it to the Bureau of Labor-Management Reports
   B. to refer it to the National Labor Relations Board
   C. to report it to the New York State Department of Labor
   D. that he has no basis for a complaint

16. A worker complains that his union's self-insured welfare fund has refused to pay him anything on his wife's doctor bills even though the printed booklet states that his family is covered for a part of such bills. 16.___
Tell him to complain to the
   A. Bureau of Labor-Management Reports
   B. National Labor Relations Board
   C. New York State Insurance Department
   D. New York State Banking Department

17. A worker makes the following complaint: *I had to go to Puerto Rico because my mother was dying. I called the foreman on the telephone the day I left and told him the story. When I arrived in Puerto Rico, I found my mother dead. I stayed for the funeral. One week later, I returned to work. The employer refused to take me back. There is no union in the shop.*
You should tell him
   A. to refer it to the National Labor Relations Board
   B. to contact the New York State Department of Labor
   C. to report it to the District Attorney
   D. that he has no valid complaint

17.___

18. A worker in a company engaged in interstate commerce complains that his employer fired him because he asked for time and a half pay for 10 of the 50 hours he worked during the week. Since the employer has no time clock, the worker kept his time records by signing in and out each day.
You should refer him to the
   A. National Labor Relations Board
   B. Bureau of Labor-Management Reports
   C. Wage and Hour and Public Contracts Division
   D. District Attorney

18.___

19. A man claims that he hurt his back as a result of work as a messenger for a retail store in New York City.
In connection with filing a complaint with the Workmen's Compensation Board, his employer may NOT
   A. contest the extent of the financial claim
   B. contest the claim on the grounds that the claimant was intoxicated
   C. refuse to sign the report of the accident for submission to the Board
   D. contest the claim on the grounds that another employee's negligence was responsible for the injury

19.___

20. A contract provides for July 4th as a holiday with pay. This year July 4th fell on a Saturday. On a previous occasion on which a contract-paid holiday fell on a Saturday, the plant worked five preceding days and the employees received 48 hours pay for the week. On this occasion, the employer shut the plant down on Friday, July 3rd, and the employees were paid 40 hours pay for that week. They complained that they were locked out on Friday, July 3rd, and were entitled to pay for the day. The union contract does not call for any particular amount of notice prior to a layoff.
You should tell the complaining workers
   A. to complain to the National Labor Relations Board
   B. to complain to the Wage and Hour and Public Contracts Division
   C. to file a grievance with the union
   D. that they have no valid complaint

20.___

21. Of the following, the group which is NOT represented by a labor union is 21.___
   A. actors B. doctors
   C. farm workers D. teachers

22. Which of the following orders may an employer submit to an employment agency when requesting that workers be referred to him? 22.___
   A. Skilled welder, male, under 50
   B. Short order cook, female, French nationality
   C. Nurse, female, white
   D. Masseur, male, 2 years previous experience

23. Which of the following statements is INCORRECT? 23.___
   A. Children under 16 years may be employed after school hours or during vacations, but not in factory work.
   B. Working papers are issued through the New York State Employment Service.
   C. Boys 12 years of age or over are permitted to deliver newspapers and magazines to homes or business places.
   D. The law makes special provisions for child performers at theatrical, television, or radio performances.

24. The Immigration and Naturalization Service is under the authority of the 24.___
   A. Department of Health, Education and Welfare
   B. Department of Justice
   C. Department of Labor
   D. Post Office Department

25. Which of the following is an example of an inequity, in the industrial relations sense of the word? 25.___
A(n)
   A. foreman bullies a worker to the point where the worker is forced to quit
   B. employer refuses to hire a man solely on account of his race
   C. machinist of 10 years' seniority is paid 10¢ an hour less than a machinist of 5 years' seniority and equal skill
   D. supervisor suspends an employee for insubordination

KEY (CORRECT ANSWERS)

1. B	6. A	11. B	16. C	21. B
2. A	7. D	12. D	17. D	22. D
3. B	8. C	13. B	18. C	23. B
4. C	9. A	14. B	19. C	24. B
5. D	10. A	15. D	20. D	25. C

Glossary of Personnel Terms

CONTENTS

Glossary of Personnel Terms

A

Abandonment of Position—When an employee quits work without resigning. (715)

Absence Without Leave (AWOL)—Absence without prior approval, therefore without pay, that may be subject to disciplinary action. See also, *Leave Without Pay,* which is an approved absence. (630)

Administrative Workweek—A period of seven consecutive calendar days designated in advance by the head of the agency. Usually an administrative workweek coincides with a calendar week. (610)

Admonishment—Informal reproval of an employee by a supervisor; usually oral, but some agencies require written notice. (751)

Adverse Action—A removal, suspension, furlough without pay for 30 days or less, or reduction-in-grade or pay. An adverse action may be taken against an employee for disciplinary or non-disciplinary reasons. However, if the employee is covered by FPM part 752, the action must be in accordance with those procedures. Removals or reductions-in-grade based solely on unacceptable performance are covered by Part 432. Actions taken for reductions-in-force reasons are covered by Part 351. (752)

Affirmative Action—A policy followed closely by the Federal civil service that requires agencies to take positive steps to insure equal opportunity in employment, development, advancement, and treatment of all employees and applicants for employment regardless of race, color, sex, religion, national origin, or physical or mental handicap. Affirmative action also requires that specific actions be directed at the special problems and unique concerns in assuring equal employment opportunity for minorities, women and other disadvantaged groups.

Agreement—See *Collective Bargaining.*

Annuitant—A retired Federal civil service employee or a survivor (spouse or children) being paid an annuity from the Retirement Fund. (831)

Annuity—Payments to a former employee who retired, or to the surviving spouse or children. It is computed as an annual rate but paid monthly. (831)

Appeal—A request by an employee for review of an agency action by an outside agency. The right to such review is provided by law or regulation and may include an adversary-type hearing and a written decision in which a finding of facts is made and applicable law, Executive order and regulations are applied.

Appointing Officer—A person having power by law or lawfully delegated authority to make appointments. (210, 311)

Appointment, Noncompetitive—Employment without competing with others, in the sense that it is done without regard to civil service registers, etc. Includes reinstatements, transfers, reassignments, demotions, and promotion. (335)

Appointment, Superior Qualifications—Appointment of a candidate to a position in grade 11 or above of the General Schedule at a rate above the minimum because of the candidate's superior qualifications. A rate above the minimum for the grade must be justified by the applicant's unusually high or unique qualifications, a special need of the Government for the candidate's services, or because the candidate's current pay is higher than the minimum for the grade which he or she is offered. (338, 531)

Appointment, TAPER—Abbreviation for "temporary appointment pending establishment of a register." Employment made under an OPM authority granted to an agency when there are insufficient eligibles on a register appropriate to fill the position involved. (316)

Appointment, Temporary Limited—Nonpermanent appointment of an employee hired for a specified time of one year or less, or for seasonal or intermittent positions. (316)

Appointment, Term—Nonpermanent appointment of an employee hired to work on a project expected to last over one year, but less than four years. (316)

Appropriate Unit— A group of employees which a labor organization seeks to represent for the purpose of negotiating agreements; an aggregation of employees which has a clear and identifiable community of interest and which promotes effective dealings and efficiency of operations. It may be established on a plant or installation, craft, functional or other basis. (Also known as bargaining unit, appropriate bargaining unit.) (711)

Arbitration—Final step of the negotiated grievance procedure which may be invoked by the agency or the union (not the employee) if the grievance has not been resolved. Involves use of an impartial arbitrator selected by the agency and union to render a binding award to resolve the grievance. (711)

Arbitrator—An impartial third party to whom disputing parties submit their differences for decision (award). An *ad hoc* arbitrator is one selected to act in a specific case or a limited group of cases. A permanent arbitrator is one selected to serve for the life of the agreement or a stipulated term, hearing all disputes that arise during this period. (711)

Area Office (OPM)—Forcal point for administering and implementing all OPM programs, except investigations, in the geographic area assigned. Provides personnel management advice and assistance to agencies, and personnel evaluation, recruiting and examining and special program leadership. Principal source of employment information for agencies and the public.

Audit, Work—Visit to an employee or his supervisor to verify or gather information about a position. Sometimes called "desk audit."

B

Bargaining Rights—Legally recognized right of the labor organization to represent employees in negotiations with employers. (711)

Bargaining Unit—An appropriate grouping of employees represented on an exclusive basis by a labor organization. "Appropriate" for this purpose means that it is a grouping of employees who share a community of interest and which promotes effective union and agency dealings and efficient agency operations. (711)

Basic Workweek—For a full-time employee, the 40-hour nonovertime work schedule within an administrative workweek. The usual workweek consists of five 8-hour days, Monday through Friday. (610)

Break in Service—The time between separation and reemployment that may cause a loss of rights or privileges. For transfer purposes, it means not being on an agency payroll for one working day or more. For the three-year career conditional period or for reinstatement purposes, it means not being on an agency payroll for over 30 calendar days. (315)

Bumping—During reduction-in-force, the displacement of one employee by another employee in a higher group or subgroup. (351)

C

Career—Tenure of a permanent employee in the competitive service who has completed three years of substantially continuous creditable Federal service. (315)

Career-Conditional—Tenure of a permanent employee in the competitive service who *has not* completed three years of substantially continuous creditable Federal service. (315)

Career Counseling—Service available to employees to assist them in: (1) assessing their skills, abilities, interests, and aptitudes; (2) determining qualifications required for occupations within the career system and how the requirements relate to their individual capabilities; (3) defining their career goals and developing plans for reaching the goals; (4) indentifying and assessing education and training opportunities and enrollment procedures; (5) identifying factors which may impair career development; and (6) learning about resources, inside or outside the agency, where additional help is available. (250)

Career Development—Systematic development designed to increase an employee's potential for advancement and career change. It may include classroom training, reading, work experience, etc. (410)

Career Ladder—A career ladder is a series of developmental positions of increasing difficulty in the same line of work, through which an employee may progress to a journeyman level on his or her personal development and performance in that series.

Career Reserved Position—A position within SES that has a specific requirement for impartiality. May be filled only by career appointment. (920)

Ceiling, Personnel—The maximum number of employees authorized at a given time. (312)

Certificate—A list of eligibles ranked, according to regulations, for appointment or promotion consideration. A more useful term is "candidate list." (332, 335)

Certification—The process by which eligibles are ranked, according to regulations, for appointment or promotion consideration. (332, 335)

Certification, Selective—Certifying only the names of eligibles who have special qualifications required to fill particular vacant positions. (332)

Certification, Top of the Register—Certifying in regular order, beginning with the eligibles at the top of the register. (332)

Change in Duty Station—A personnel action that changes an employee from one geographical location to another in the same agency. (296)

Change to Lower Grade—Downgrading a position or reducing an employee's grade. See Demotion. (296)

Class of Positions—All positions sufficiently similar in: (1) kind or subject matter of work; (2) level of difficulty and responsibility; and (3) qualification requirements, so as to warrant similar treatment in personnel and pay administration. For example, all Grade GS-3 Clerk-Typist positions. (511)

Classified Service—See *Competitive Service* (212)

Collective Bargaining—Performance of the mutual obligation of the employer and the exclusive (employee) representative to meet at reasonable times, to confer and negotiate in good faith, and to execute a written agreement with respect to conditions of employment, except that by any such obligation neither party shall be compelled to agree to proposals, or be required to make concessions. (Also known as collective negotiations, negotiations, and negotiation of agreement.) (711)

Collective Bargaining Agreement—A written agreement between management and a labor organization which is usually for a definite term, and usually defines conditions of employment, and includes grievance and arbitration procedures. The terms "collective bargaining agreement" and "contract" are synonymous. (711)

Collective Bargaining Unit—A group of employees recognized as appropriate for representation by a labor organization for collective bargaining. (See *Appropriate Unit*) (711)

Compensatory Time Off—Time off (hour-for-hour) granted an employee in lieu of overtime pay. (550)

Competitive Area—For reduction-in-force, that part of an agency within which employees are in competition for retention. Generally, it is that part of an agency covered by a single appointing office. (351)

Competitive Service—Federal positions normally filled through open competitive examination (hence the term "competitive service") under civil service rules and regulations. About 86 percent of all Federal positions are in the competitive service. (212)

Competitive Status—Basic eligibility of a person to be selected to fill a position in the competitive service without open competitive examination. Competitive status may be acquired by career-conditional or career appointment through open competitive examination, or may be granted by statute, executive order, or civil service rules without competitive examination. A person with competitive status may be promoted, transferred, reassigned, reinstated, or demoted subject to the conditions prescribed by civil service rules and regulations. (212)

Consultant—An advisor to an officer or instrumentality of the Government, as distinguished from an officer or employee who carries out the agency's duties and responsibilities. (304)

Consultation—The obligation of an agency to consult the labor organization on particular personnel issues. The process of consultation lies between notification to the labor organization, which may amount simply to providing information, and negotiation, which implies agreement on the part of the labor organization. (711)

Conversion—The process of changing a person's tenure from one type of appointment to another (e.g., conversion from temporary to career-conditional). (315)

D

Demotion—A change of an employee, while serving continuously with the same agency:

(a) To a lower grade when both the old and the new positions are in the General Schedule or under the same type graded wage schedule; or

(b) To a position with a lower rate of pay when both the old and the new positions are under the same type ungraded wage schedule, or are in different pay method categories. (335, 752)

Detail—A temporary assignment of an employee to different duties or to a different position for a specified time, with the employee returning to his/her regular duties at the end of the detail. (300)

Differentials—Recruiting incentives in the form of compensation adjustments justified by: (1) extraordinarily difficult living conditions; (2) excessive physical hardship; or (3) notably unhealthful conditions. (591)

Disciplinary Action—Action taken to correct the conduct of an employee; may range from an admonishment through reprimand, suspension, reduction in grade or pay, to removal from the service. (751, 752)

Displaced Employee Program—(DEP)—A system to help find jobs for career and career-conditional employees displaced either through reduction-in-force or by an inability to accept assignment to another commuting area. (330)

Downgrading—Change of a position to a lower grade. (511, 532)

Dual Compensation—When an employee receives compensation for more than one Federal position if he/she worked more than 40 hours during the week. The term is also used in connection with compensation from a full-time Federal position as well as a retirement annuity for prior military service. (550)

Duty Station—The specific geographical area in which an employee is permanently assigned. (296)

E

Eligible—Any applicant for appointment or promotion who meets the minimum qualification requirements. (337)

Employee Development—A term which may include *career development* and *upward mobility*. It may be oriented toward development for better performance on an employee's current job, for learning a new policy or procedure, or for enchancing an employee's potential for advancement. (410, 412)

Employee, Exempt—An employee exempt from the overtime provisions of the Fair Labor Standards Act. (551)

Employee, Nonexempt—An employee subject to the overtime provision of the Fair Labor Standards Act. (551)

Employee Organization —See *Labor Organization.*

Employee Relations—The personnel function which centers upon the relationship between the supervisor and individual employees. (711)

Entrance Level Position—A position in an occupation at the beginning level grade. (511)

Environmental Differential—Additional pay authorized for a duty involving unusally severe hazards or working conditions. (532, 550)

Equal Employment Opportunity—Federal policy to provide equal employment opportunity for all; to prohibit discrimination on the grounds of age, race, color, religion, sex, national origin, or physical or mental handicap; and to promote the full realization of employees' potential through a continuing affirmative action program in each executive department and agency. (713)

Equal Employment Opportunity Commission—Regulates and enforces the Federal program for insuring equal employment opportunity, and oversees the development and implementation of Federal agencies' affirmative action programs.

Equal Pay for Substantially Equal Work—An underlying principle that provides the same pay level for work at the same level of difficulty and responsibility. (271)

Examination—A means of measuring, in a practical and suitable manner, qualifications of applicants for employment in specific positions. (337)

Examination, Assembled—An examination which includes as one of its parts a written or performance test for which applicants are required to assemble at appointed times and places. (337)

Examination, Fitness-For-Duty—An agency directed examination given by a Federal medical officer or an employee-designated, agency-approved physician to determine the employee's physical, mental, or emotional ability to perform assigned duties safely and efficiently. (339, 831)

Examination, Unassembled—An examination in which applicants are rated on their education, experience, and other qualifications as shown in the formal application and any supportive evidence that may be required, without assembling for a written or performance test. (337)

Excepted Service—Positions in the Federal civil service not subject to the appointment requirements of the competitive service. Exceptions to the normal, competitive requirements are authorized by law, executive order, or regulation. (213, 302)

Exclusive Recognition—The status conferred on a labor organization which receives a majority of votes cast in a representation election, entitling it to act for and negotiate agreements covering all employees included in an appropriate bargaining unit. The labor organization enjoying this status is known as the exclusive representative, exclusive bargaining representative, bargaining agent, or exclusive bargaining agent. (711)

Executive Inventory—An OPM computerized file which contains background information on all members of the Senior Executive Service and persons in positions at GS-16 through GS-18 or the equivalent, and individuals at lower grades who have been certified as meeting the managerial criteria for SES. It is used as an aid to agencies in executive recruiting and as a planning and management tool. (920)

Executive Resources Board—Panel of top agency executives responsible under the law for conducting the merit staffing process for career appointment to Senior Executive Service (SES) positions in the agency. Most Boards are also responsible for setting policy on and overseeing such areas as SES position planning and executive development. (920)

F

Federal Labor Relations Authority (FLRA)—Administers the Federal service labor-management relations program. It resolves questions of union representation of employees; prosecutes and adjudicates allegations of unfair labor practices; decides questions of what is or is not negotiable; and on appeal, reviews decisions of arbitrators. (5 USC 7104)

Federal Personnel Manual (FPM)—The official publication containing Federal personnel regulations and guidance. Also contains the code of Federal civil service law, selected Executive orders pertaining to Federal employment, and civil service rules. (171)

Federal Service Impasses Panel (FSIP)—Administrative body created to resolve bargaining impasses in the Federal service. The Panel may recommend procedures, including arbitration, for settling impasses, or may settle the impasse itself. Considered the legal alternative to strike in the Federal sector. (711)

Federal Wage System (FWS)—A body of laws and regulations governing the administrative processes related to trades and laboring occupations in the Federal service. (532)

Full Field Investigation—Personal investigation of an applicant's background to determine whether he/she meets fitness standards for a critical-sensitive Federal position. (736)

Function—All, or a clearly identifiable segment, of an agency's mission, including all the parts of that mission, (e.g., procurement), regardless of how performed. (351)

G

General Position—A position within the Senior Executive Service that may be filled by a career, noncareer, or limited appointment. (920)

General Schedule—(GS)—The graded pay system as presented by Chapter 51 of Title 5, United States Code, for classifying positions. (511)

Grade—All classes of positions which, although different with respect to kind or subject matter of work, are sufficiently equivalent as to (1) level of difficulty and responsibility, and (2) level of qualification requirements of the work to warrant the inclusion of such classes of positions within one range of rates of basic compensation. (511, 532)

Grade Retention—The right of a General Schedule or prevailing rate employee, when demoted for certain reasons, to retain the higher grade for most purposes for two years. (536)

Grievance, (Negotiated Procedure)—Any complaint or expressed dissatisfaction by an employee against an action by management in connection with his job, pay or other aspects of employment. Whether such complaint or expressed dissatisfaction is formally recognized and handled as a "grievance" under a negotiated procedure depends on the scope of that procedure. (711)

Grievance (Under Agency Administrative Procedure)—A request by an employee or by a group of employees acting as individuals, for personal relief in a matter of concern or dissatisfaction to the employee, subject to the control of agency management.

Grievance Procedure—A procedure, either administrative or negotiated, by which employees may seek redress of any matter subject to the control of agency management. (711, 771)

H

Handbook X-118—The official qualification standards manual for General Schedule Positions. (338)

Handbook X-118C—The official qualification standards manual for Wage System positions. (338)

Hearing—The opportunity for contending parties under a grievance, complaint, or other remedial process, to introduce testimony and evidence and to confront and examine or cross examine witnesses. (713, 771, 772)

I

Impasse Procedures—Procedures for resolving deadlocks between agencies and union in collective bargaining. (711)

Incentive Awards—An all-inclusive term covering awards granted under Part 451 or OPM regulations. Includes an award for a suggestion submitted by an employee and adopted by management; a special achievement award for performance exeeding job requirements, or an honorary award in the form of a certificate, emblem, pin or other item. (451)

Indefinite—Tenure of a nonpermanent employee hired for an unlimited time. (316)

Injury, Work Related—For compensation under the Federal Employees' Compensation Act, a personal injury sustained while in the performance of duty. The term "injury" includes diseases proximately caused by the employment. (810)

Injury, Traumatic—Under the Federal Employees' Compensation Act, for continuation of pay purposes, a wound or other condition of the body caused by external force, including stress or strain. The injury must be identifiable by time and place of occurrence and member or function of the body affected, and be caused by a specific event or incident or series of events or incidents within a single day or work shift. (810)

Intergovernmental Personnel Assignment—Assignments of personnel to and from the Executive Branch of the Federal Government, state and local government agencies, and institutions of higher education up to two years, although a two-year extension may be permitted. The purpose is to provide technical assistance or expertise where needed for short periods of time. (334)

Intermittent—Less than full-time employment requiring irregular work hours which cannot be prescheduled. (610)

J

Job Analysis—Technical review and evaluation of a position's duties, responsibilities, and level of work and of the skills, abilities, and knowledge needed to do the work. (511, 532)

Job Enrichment—Carefully planned work assignments and/or training to use and upgrade employee skills, abilities, and interests; and to provide opportunity for growth, and encourage self-improvement. (312)

Job Freeze—A restriction on hiring and/or promotion by administrative or legislative action. (330)

Job Title—The formal name of a position as determined by official classification standards. (511, 532)

Journeyman Level—(Full Performance Level)—The lowest level of a career ladder position at which an employee has learned the full range of duties in a specific occupation. All jobs below full performance level are developmental levels, through which each employee in the occupation may progress to full performance. (511)

L

Labor-Management Relations—Relationships and dealings between employee unions and management. (711)

Labor Organization—An organization composed in whole or in part of employees, in which employees participate and pay dues, and which has as a purpose dealing with an agency concerning grievances and working conditions of employment. (711)

Lead Agency—Under the Federal Wage System, the Federal agency with the largest number of Federal wage workers in a geographical area; consequently, it has the primary role for determining wage rates for all Federal employees who work in that area and are covered by the System. (532)

Leave, Annual—Time allowed to employees for vacation and other absences for personal reasons. (630)

Leave, Court—Time allowed to employees for jury and certain types of witness service. (630)

Leave, Military—Time allowed to employees for certain types of military service. (630)

Leave, Sick—Time allowed to employees for physical incapacity, to prevent the spread of contagious diseases, or to obtain medical, dental or eye examination or treatment. (630)

Leave Without Pay (LWOP)—A temporary nonpay status and absence from duty, requested by an employee. The permissive nature of "leave without pay" distinguishes it from "absence without leave." (630)

Level of Difficulty—A classification term used to indicate the relative ranking of duties and responsibilities. (511, 532)

M

Maintenance Review—A formal, periodic review (usually annual) of all positions in an organization, or portion of an organization, to insure that classifications are correct and position descriptions are current. (511)

Major Duty—Any duty or responsibility, or group of closely related tasks, of a position which (1) determines qualification requirements for the position, (2) occupies a significant amount of the employee's time, and (3) is a regular or recurring duty. (511)

Management Official—An individual employed by an agency in a position whose duties and responsibilities require or authorize the individual to formulate, determine or influence the policies of the agency. (711)

Management Rights—The right of management to make day-to-day personnel decisions and to direct the work force without mandatory negotiation with the exclusive representative. (See "Reserved Rights Doctrine.") Usually a specific list of management authorities not subject to the obligation to bargain. (117)

Mediation—Procedure using a third-party to facilitate the reaching of an agreement voluntarily. (711)

Merit Promotion Program—The system under which agencies consider an employee for internal personnel actions on the basis of personal merit. (335)

Merit Systems Protection Board (MSPB)—An independent agency which monitors the administration of the Federal civil service system, prosecutes and adjudicates allegations of merit principle abuses, and hears and decides other civil service appeals. (5 USC 1205)

N

National Agency Check and Inquiry (NACI)—The Investigation of applicants for nonsensitive Federal positions by means of a name check through national investigative files and voucher inquiries. (731)

National Consultation Rights—A relationship established between the headquarters of a Federal agency and the national office of a union under criteria of the Federal Labor Relations Authority. When a union holds national consultation rights, the agency must give the union notice of proposed new substantive personnel policies, and of proposed changes in personnel policies, and an opportunity to comment on such proposals. The union has a right to: (1) suggest changes in personnel policies and have those suggestions carefully considered; (2) consult at reasonable times with appropriate officials about personnel policy matters; and (3) submit its views in writing on personnel policy matters at any time. The agency must provide the union with a written statement (which need not be detailed) of reasons for taking its final action on a policy. (711)

Negotiability—A determination as to whether a matter is within the obligation to bargain. (711)

Negotiated Grievance Procedure—A procedure applicable to members of a bargaining unit for considering grievances. Coverage and scope are negotiated by the parties to the agreement, except that the procedures may not cover certain matters designated in Title VII of the CSRA as excluded from the scope of negotiated grievance procedures. (711)

Negotiations—The bargaining process used to reach a settlement between labor and management over conditions of employment. (711)

Nominating Officer—A subordinate officer of an agency to whom authority has been delegated by the head of the agency to nominate for appointment but not actually appoint employees. (311)

O

Objection—A written statement by an agency of the reasons why it believes an eligible whose name is on a certificate is not qualified for the position to which referred. If the Examining Office sustains the objection, the agency may eliminate the person from consideration. (332)

Occupational Group—Positions of differing kinds but within the same field of work. For example, the GS-500 Accounting and Budget Occupational Group includes: General Accounting Clerical and Administrative Series; Financial Management; Internal Revenue Agent Accounting Technician; Payroll; etc. (511, 532)

Office of Personnel Management (OPM)—Regulates, administers, and evaluates the civil service program according to merit principles. (5 USC 1103)

Office of Workers Compensation Programs (OWCP)—In the Department of Labor, administers statutes that allow compensation to employees and their survivors for work-related injuries and illnesses. Decides and pays claims. (810)

Official Personnel Folder (OPF)—The official repository of employment records and documents affecting personnel actions during an employee's Federal civilian service. (293)

Overtime Work—Under Title 5, U.S. Code, officially ordered or approved work performed in excess of eight hours in a day or 40 hours in a week. Under the Fair Labor Standards Act, work in excess of 40 hours in a week by a nonexempt employee. (550, 551)

P

Pass Over—Elimination from appointment consideration of a veteran preference eligible on a certificate (candidate list), to appoint a lower ranking nonveteran, when the agency submits reasons which OPM finds sufficient. (332)

Pay Retention—The right of a General Schedule or prevailing rate employee (following a grade retention period or at other specified times when the rate of basic pay would otherwise be reduced) to continue to receive the higher rate. Pay is retained indefinitely. (536)

Pay, Severance—Money paid to employees separated by reduction-in-force and not eligible for retirement. The following formula is used, but the amount cannot be more than one year's pay:

Basic Severance Pay—One week's pay for each year of civilian service up to 10 years, and two weeks' pay for each year served over 10 years, plus

Age Adjustment Allowance—10 percent of the basic severance pay for each year over age 40. (550)

Performance Appraisal—The comparison, under a performance appraisal system, of an employee's actual performance against the performance standards previously established for the position. (430)

Personnel Action—The process necessary to appoint, separate, reinstate, or make other changes affecting an employee (e.g., change in position assignment, tenure, etc.). (296)

Personnel Management—Management of human resources to accomplish a mission and provide individual job satisfaction. It is the line responsibility of the operating supervisor and the staff responsibility of the personnel office. (250)

Position—A specific job consisting of all the current major duties and responsibilities assigned or delegated by management. (312)

Position Change—A promotion, demotion, or reassignment. (335)

Position Classification—Analyzing and categorizing jobs by occupational group, series, class, and grade according to like duties, responsibilities, and qualification requirements. (511, 532)

Position Classifier—A specialist in job analysis who determines the titles, occupational groups, series, and grades of positions. (312)

Position Description—An official written statement of the major duties, responsibilities and supervisory relationships of a position. (312)

Position Management—The process of designing positions to combine logical and consistent duties and responsibilities into an orderly, efficient, and productive organization to accomplish agency mission. (312)

Position Survey—Agency review of positions to determine whether the positions are still needed and, if so, whether the classification and position description are correct. (312)

Position, "PL 313 Type"—Positions established under Public Law 80-313 of August 1, 1947, or similar authorities. A small group of high level professional and scientific positions generally in the competitive service, but not filled through competitive examinations. Salaries are set between GS-12 and GS-18. (534)

Preference, Compensable Disability ("CP")—Ten-point preference awarded to a veteran separated under honorable conditions from active duty, who receives compensation of 10 percent or more for a service-connected disability. Eligible "CP" veterans are placed at the top of civil service lists of eligibles for positions at GS-9 or higher. (211)

Preference, 30 Percent or More, Disabled ("CPS")—A disabled veteran whose disability is rated at 30 percent or more, entitled to special preference in appointment and during reduction in force.

Preference, Disability ("XP")—Ten-point preference in hiring for a veteran separated under honorable conditions from active duty and who has a service-connected disability or receives compensation, pension, or disability retirement from the VA or a uniformed service. (211)

Preference, Mother ("XP")—Ten-point preference to which the mother of a deceased or disabled military veteran may be entitled. (211)

Preference, Spouse ("XP")—Ten-point preference to which a disabled military veteran's spouse may be entitled. (211)

Preference, Tentative ("TP")—Five-point veteran preference tentatively awarded an eligible who served on active duty during specified periods and was separated from military service under honorable conditions. It must be verified by the appointing officer. (211)

Preference, Veteran—The statutory right to special advantage in appointments or separations; based on a person's discharge under honorable conditions from the armed forces, for a service-connected disability. *Not* applicable to the Senior Executive Service. (211)

Preference, Widow or Widower ("XP")—Ten-point preference to which a military veteran's widow or widower may be entitled. (211)

Premium Pay—Additional pay for overtime, night, Sunday and holiday work. (550)

Prevailing Rate System—A subsystem of the Federal Wage System used to determine the employee's pay in a particular wage area. The determination requires comparing the rate of pay with the private sector for similar duties and responsibilities. (532)

Probationary Period—A trial period which is a condition of the initial competitive appointment. Provides the final indispensable test of ability, that of actual performance on the job. (315)

Promotion—A change of an employee to a higher grade when both the old and new positions are under the same job classification system and pay schedule, or to a position with higher pay in a different job classification system and pay schedule. (335)

Promotion, Career—Promotion of an employee without current competition when: (1) he/she had earlier been competitively selected from a register or under competitive promotion procedures for an assignment intended as a matter of record to be preparation for the position being filled; or (2) the position is reconstituted at a higher grade because of additional duties and responsibilities. (335)

Promotion, Competitive—Selection of a current or former Federal civil service employee for a higher grade position, using procedures that compare the candidates on merit. (335)

Promotion Certificate—A list of best qualified candidates to be considered to fill a position under competitive promotion procedures. (335)

Q

Qualifications Review Board—A panel attached to OPM that determines whether a candidate for career appointment in the Senior Executive Service meets the managerial criteria established by law.

Qualification Requirements—Education, experience, and other prerequisites to employment or placement in a position. (338)

Quality Graduate—College graduate who was a superior student and can be hired at a higher grade than the one to which he/she would otherwise be entitled. (338)

Quality Increase—An additional within-grade increase granted to General Schedule employees for high quality performance above that ordinarily found in the type of position concerned (531).

R

Reassignment—The change of an employee, while serving continuously within the same agency, from one position to another, without promotion or demotion. (210)

Recognition—Employer acceptance of a labor organization as authorized to negotiate, usually for all members of a bargaining unit. (711) Also, used to refer to incentive awards granted under provisions of Parts 451 and 541 of OPM Regulations, and Quality Increases granted under Part 531.

Recruitment—Process of attracting a supply of qualified eligibles for employment consideration. (332)

Reduction-in-Force (RIF)—A personnel action that may be required due to lack of work or funds, changes resulting from reorganization, downward reclassification of a position, or the need to make room for an employee with reemployment or restoration rights. Involves separating an employee from his/her present position, but does not necessarily result in separation or downgrading. (351) (See also *Tenure Groups.*)

Reemployment Priority List—Career and career-conditional employees, separated by reduction-in-force, who are identified, in priority order, for reemployment to competitive positions in the agency in the commuting area where the separations occurred. (330)

Reemployment Rights—Right of an employee to return to an agency after detail, transfer, or appointment to: (1) another Executive agency during an emergency; (2) an internation organiization; or (3) other statutorily covered employment, e.g., the Peace Corps. (352)

Register—A list of eligible applicants compiled in the order of their relative standing for referral to Federal jobs, after competitive civil service examination. (332,210)

Reinstatement—Noncompetitive reemployment in the competitive service based on previous service under a career or career-conditional appointment. (315)

Removal—Separation of an employee for cause or because of continual unacceptable performance. (432, 752)

Representation—Actions and rights of the labor organization to consult and negotiate with management on behalf of the bargaining unit and represent employees in the unit. (711)

Representation Election—Election conducted to determine whether the employees in an appropriate unit (See *Bargaining Unit*) desire a labor organization to act as their exclusive representative. (711)

Reprimand—An official rebuke of an employee. Normally in writing and placed in the temporary side of an employee's OPF-(751)

"Reserved Rights Doctrine"—Specific functions delegated to management by Title VII of CSRA that protect management's ability to perform its necessary functions and duties. (See Management Rights.) Delegates to management specific functions not subject to negotiation except as to procedures and impact. (711)

Resignation—A separation, prior to retirement, in response to an employee's request for the action. It is a voluntary expression of the employee's desire to leave the organization and must not be demanded as an alternative to some other action to be taken or withheld. (715)

Restoration Rights—Employees who enter military service or sustain a compensable job-related injury or disability are entitled to be restored to the same or higher employment status held prior to their absence. (353)

Retention Preference—The relative standing of employees competing in a reduction-in-force. Their standing is determined by veterans preference, tenure group, length of service, and performance appraisal. (351)

Retention Register—A list of all employees, arranged by competitive level, describing their retention preference during reductions-in-force. (351)

Retirement—Payment of an annuity after separation from a position under the Civil Service Retirement System and based on meeting age and length of service requirements. The types of retirement are:

Deferred—An employee with five years civilian service who separates or transfers to a position not under the Retirement Act, may receive an annuity at age 62, if he/she does not withdraw from the Retirement Fund. (831)

Disability—An immediate annuity paid to an employee under the retirement system who has completed five years of civilian service and has suffered a mental, emotional, or physical disability not the result of the employee's vicious habits, intemperance, or willful misconduct. (831)

Discontinued Service—An immediate annuity paid to an employee who is involuntarily separated, through no personal fault of the employee, after age 50 and 20 years of service, or at any age with 25 years of service. This annuity is reduced by 1/6 of one percent for each full month under age 55 (two percent per year). (831)

Optional—The minimum combinations of age and service for this kind of immediate annuity are: age 62 with five years of service; age 60 with 20 years of service; age 55 with 30 years of service. (831)

Review, Classification—An official written request for reclassification of a position. Previously called a classification appeal.

S

Schedules A, B, and C—Categories of positions excepted from the competitive service by regulation. (213)

Schedule A—Positions other than confidential or policy

determining, for which it is not practical to examine.
Schedule B—Positions other than confidential or policy determining for which it is not practical to hold a competitive examination.
Schedule C—Positions of a confidential or policy determining character.

Senior Executive Service—A separate personnel system for persons who set policy and administer programs at the top levels of the Government (equivalent to GS-16 through Executive Level IV). (920)

Service Computation Date-Leave—The date, either actual or adjusted, from which service credit is accumulated for determining the rate of leave accrual; it may be different from the service computation date, which determines relative standing in a subgroup for reduction-in-force, or service computation date for retirement. (296)

Service Record Card (Standard Form 7)—A brief of the employee's service history. It is kept on file in accordance with agency disposition instructions. (295)

Special Salary Rates—Salary rates higher than regular statutory schedule; established for occupations in which private enterprise pays substantially more than the regular Federal Schedule. (530)

Spoils System—The personnel system characterized by the political appointment and removal of employees without regard to merit. (212)

Staffing—Use of available and projected personnel through recruitment, appointment, reassignment, promotion, reduction-in-force, etc., to provide the work force required to fulfill the agency's mission. (250)

Standard Form 171 ("Personal Qualification Statement")—Used in applying for a Federal position through a competitive examination. (295)

Standards of Conduct For Labor Organization—In the Federal sector, a code governing internal democratic practices and fiscal responsibility, and procedures to which a labor organization must adhere to be eligible to receive any recognition. (711)

Steward (Union Steward)—A local union's representative in a plant or department, appointed by the union to carry out union duties, adjust grievances, collect dues and solicit new members. Stewards are employees trained by the union to carry out their duties.

Strike—Temporary stoppage of work by a group of employees to express a grievance, enforce a demand for changes in conditions of employment, obtain recognition, or resolve a dispute with management. *Wildcat strike*—a strike not sanctioned by union and which may violate a collective agreement. *Quickie strike*—a spontaneous or unannounced strike of short duration. *Slowdown*—a deliberate reduction of output without an actual strike in order to force concessions from an employer. *Walkout*—same as strike. Strikes are illegal for Federal employees. (711)

Suitability—An applicant's or employee's fitness for Federal employment as indicated by character and conduct. (731)

Supervisor—An individual employed by an agency having authority, in the interest of the agency, to hire, direct, assign, promote, reward, transfer, furlough, lay off, recall, suspend, discipline or remove employees, to adjust their grievances, or to effectively recommend such action—if the exercise of the authority is not merely routine or clerical in nature but requires the consistent exercise of independent judgement. With respect to any unit which includes firefighters or nurses, the term "supervisor" includes only those individuals who devote a preponderance of their employment time to exercising such authority. (711).

Survey, Classification—An intensive study of all positions in an organization or organizational segment to insure their correct classification.

Suspension—Placing an employee, for disciplinary reasons, in a temporary status without duties and pay. (751, 752)

T

Tenure—The time an employee may reasonably expect to serve under a current appointment. It is governed by the type of appointment, without regard to whether the employee has competitive status. (210)

Tenure Groups—Categories of employees ranked in priority order for retention during reduction-in-force. Within each group, veterans are ranked above nonveterans. For the competitive service, the tenure groups are, in descending order:

Group I—Employees under career appointments and not serving probation.

Group II—Employees serving probation, career-conditional employees, and career employees in obligated positions.

Group III—Employees with indefinite appointments, status quo employees under any other nonstatus, nontemporary appointment. (351)

For the *excepted service,* they are in descending order:

Group 1—Permanent employees, not serving a trial period, whose appointments carry no restriction or condition, such as "indefinite" or "time-limited".

Group II—Employees serving trial periods, those whose tenure is indefinite because they occupy obligated positions, and those whose tenure is equivalent to career-conditional in the competitive service.

Group III—Employees whose tenure is indefinite, but not potentially permanent, and temporary employees who have completed one year of current continuous employment. (351)

Tenure Subgroups—The ranking of veterans above nonveterans in each tenure group, as follows:

Subgroup AD—Veterans with service-connected disability of 30% or more.

Subgroup A—All other veterans

Subgroup B—Nonveterans

Time-in-Grade Restriction—A requirement intended to prevent excessively rapid promotions in the General Schedule. Generally, an employee may not be promoted more than two grades within one year to positions up to GS-5. At GS-5 and above, an employee must serve a minimum of one year in grade, and cannot be promoted more than one grade, or two grades if that is the normal progression. (300)

Tour of Duty—The hours of a day (a daily tour of duty) and the day of an administrative workweek (weekly tour of duty) scheduled in advance and during which an employee is required to work regularly. (610)

Training—Formal instruction or controlled and planned exposure to learning. (410)

Transfer—A change of an employee, without a break in service of one full workday, from a position in one agency to a position in another agency. (315)

Transfer of Function—For reduction-in-force, the transfer of a continuing function from one agency or competitive area to another, or when the competitive area in which work is performed is moved to another commuting area. (315)

U

Unemployment Compensation—Income maintenance payments to former Federal employees who: (1) are unemployed; (2) file a claim at a local employment office for unemployment compensation; and (3) register for work assignment. The program is administered through state and D.C. employment service offices, which determine eligibility and make the payments. (850)

Unfair Labor Practices—Prohibited actions by agency management and labor organizations. (711)

Union—See *Labor Organization.*

Upward Mobility—Systematic career development requiring competitive selection in positions that provide experience and training leading to future assignments in other, more responsible positions. (410)

V

Veteran—A person entitled to preference under 5 USC 2108, including a spouse, widow, widower, or mother entitled to preference under the law. (211)

Voucher—In staffing terms, a formal inquiry to employers, references, professors, and others who presumably know a job applicant well enough to describe job qualifications and personal character. (337)

W

Wage Employees—Those employees in trades, crafts, or labor occupations covered by the Federal Wage System, whose pay is fixed and adjusted periodically in accordance with prevailing rates. (532)

Within-Grade Increase—A salary increase provided in certain Government pay plans based upon time-in-grade and acceptable or satisfactory work performance. Also known as "periodic increase" or "step increase." (531)

NOTE:
Numbers in parentheses after the definitions refer to the appropriate FEDERAL PERSONNEL MANUAL (FPM) Chapter indicated.

ANSWER SHEET

TEST NO. ________ PART ______ TITLE OF POSITION ________________________
(AS GIVEN IN EXAMINATION ANNOUNCEMENT - INCLUDE OPTION, IF ANY)

PLACE OF EXAMINATION ______________ (CITY OR TOWN) ______________ (STATE) DATE ________

RATING

USE THE SPECIAL PENCIL. MAKE GLOSSY BLACK MARKS.

1 A B C D E	26 A B C D E	51 A B C D E	76 A B C D E	101 A B C D E
2 A B C D E	27 A B C D E	52 A B C D E	77 A B C D E	102 A B C D E
3 A B C D E	28 A B C D E	53 A B C D E	78 A B C D E	103 A B C D E
4 A B C D E	29 A B C D E	54 A B C D E	79 A B C D E	104 A B C D E
5 A B C D E	30 A B C D E	55 A B C D E	80 A B C D E	105 A B C D E
6 A B C D E	31 A B C D E	56 A B C D E	81 A B C D E	106 A B C D E
7 A B C D E	32 A B C D E	57 A B C D E	82 A B C D E	107 A B C D E
8 A B C D E	33 A B C D E	58 A B C D E	83 A B C D E	108 A B C D E
9 A B C D E	34 A B C D E	59 A B C D E	84 A B C D E	109 A B C D E
10 A B C D E	35 A B C D E	60 A B C D E	85 A B C D E	110 A B C D E

Make only ONE mark for each answer. Additional and stray marks may be counted as mistakes. In making corrections, erase errors COMPLETELY.

11 A B C D E	36 A B C D E	61 A B C D E	86 A B C D E	111 A B C D E
12 A B C D E	37 A B C D E	62 A B C D E	87 A B C D E	112 A B C D E
13 A B C D E	38 A B C D E	63 A B C D E	88 A B C D E	113 A B C D E
14 A B C D E	39 A B C D E	64 A B C D E	89 A B C D E	114 A B C D E
15 A B C D E	40 A B C D E	65 A B C D E	90 A B C D E	115 A B C D E
16 A B C D E	41 A B C D E	66 A B C D E	91 A B C D E	116 A B C D E
17 A B C D E	42 A B C D E	67 A B C D E	92 A B C D E	117 A B C D E
18 A B C D E	43 A B C D E	68 A B C D E	93 A B C D E	118 A B C D E
19 A B C D E	44 A B C D E	69 A B C D E	94 A B C D E	119 A B C D E
20 A B C D E	45 A B C D E	70 A B C D E	95 A B C D E	120 A B C D E
21 A B C D E	46 A B C D E	71 A B C D E	96 A B C D E	121 A B C D E
22 A B C D E	47 A B C D E	72 A B C D E	97 A B C D E	122 A B C D E
23 A B C D E	48 A B C D E	73 A B C D E	98 A B C D E	123 A B C D E
24 A B C D E	49 A B C D E	74 A B C D E	99 A B C D E	124 A B C D E
25 A B C D E	50 A B C D E	75 A B C D E	100 A B C D E	125 A B C D E

ANSWER SHEET

TEST NO. ______________ PART ______ TITLE OF POSITION ________________________________
(AS GIVEN IN EXAMINATION ANNOUNCEMENT - INCLUDE OPTION, IF ANY)

PLACE OF EXAMINATION ______________________________ DATE ______________
(CITY OR TOWN) (STATE)

RATING

USE THE SPECIAL PENCIL. MAKE GLOSSY BLACK MARKS.

1 A B C D E	26 A B C D E	51 A B C D E	76 A B C D E	101 A B C D E
2 A B C D E	27 A B C D E	52 A B C D E	77 A B C D E	102 A B C D E
3 A B C D E	28 A B C D E	53 A B C D E	78 A B C D E	103 A B C D E
4 A B C D E	29 A B C D E	54 A B C D E	79 A B C D E	104 A B C D E
5 A B C D E	30 A B C D E	55 A B C D E	80 A B C D E	105 A B C D E
6 A B C D E	31 A B C D E	56 A B C D E	81 A B C D E	106 A B C D E
7 A B C D E	32 A B C D E	57 A B C D E	82 A B C D E	107 A B C D E
8 A B C D E	33 A B C D E	58 A B C D E	83 A B C D E	108 A B C D E
9 A B C D E	34 A B C D E	59 A B C D E	84 A B C D E	109 A B C D E
10 A B C D E	35 A B C D E	60 A B C D E	85 A B C D E	110 A B C D E

Make only ONE mark for each answer. Additional and stray marks may be counted as mistakes. In making corrections, erase errors COMPLETELY.

11 A B C D E	36 A B C D E	61 A B C D E	86 A B C D E	111 A B C D E
12 A B C D E	37 A B C D E	62 A B C D E	87 A B C D E	112 A B C D E
13 A B C D E	38 A B C D E	63 A B C D E	88 A B C D E	113 A B C D E
14 A B C D E	39 A B C D E	64 A B C D E	89 A B C D E	114 A B C D E
15 A B C D E	40 A B C D E	65 A B C D E	90 A B C D E	115 A B C D E
16 A B C D E	41 A B C D E	66 A B C D E	91 A B C D E	116 A B C D E
17 A B C D E	42 A B C D E	67 A B C D E	92 A B C D E	117 A B C D E
18 A B C D E	43 A B C D E	68 A B C D E	93 A B C D E	118 A B C D E
19 A B C D E	44 A B C D E	69 A B C D E	94 A B C D E	119 A B C D E
20 A B C D E	45 A B C D E	70 A B C D E	95 A B C D E	120 A B C D E
21 A B C D E	46 A B C D E	71 A B C D E	96 A B C D E	121 A B C D E
22 A B C D E	47 A B C D E	72 A B C D E	97 A B C D E	122 A B C D E
23 A B C D E	48 A B C D E	73 A B C D E	98 A B C D E	123 A B C D E
24 A B C D E	49 A B C D E	74 A B C D E	99 A B C D E	124 A B C D E
25 A B C D E	50 A B C D E	75 A B C D E	100 A B C D E	125 A B C D E